Machine
APPLIQUÉ
Made Easy

Jan Brooke

NEW
HOLLAND

ACKNOWLEDGEMENTS

This book would not have been possible without the constant support of my husband Peter and son Daniel, who lived in complete disarray for the duration, as well as the encouragement and support from my good friends Betwyn Craig and Trish Knowler.

Thanks also to my wonderful and patient models, Danielle Craig, Megan Turrel, Nina Spindler and Sheridan Cheers, my son Daniel, Steven Fejes, Gary Lobegeier and Stuart Craig. They took lifeless pieces of fabric and made them come alive. I thank you for your endless patience and time.

My husband receives special thanks for his good humour and patience while he took endless photographs and also Daniel for his creative effort in designing the frog from the boy's quilt. I also thank the Knowler, Craig and Cheers families for the use of their lovely gardens and homes for the photography.

I would also like to thank Coats Paton for providing the embroidery details from their **Semco Embroidery Stitches** book.

Jan Brooke

First published in the United Kingdom in 1989 by New Holland (Publishers)
37 Connaught Street, London W2 2AZ

Originally published by
Child & Associates Publishing Pty Ltd,
5 Skyline Place, Frenchs Forest, NSW, Australia, 2086
A wholly owned Australian publishing company
This book has been edited, designed and typeset
in Australia by the Publisher
Text by Jan Brooke
© Jan Brooke 1988, 1989
Printed in Hong Kong by South Sea International Press Ltd
Typesetting processed by Deblaere Typesetting Pty Ltd

ISBN 1–85368–059–1

AUTHOR'S NOTE

The art of appliqué has become a popular craft in recent years but because there were so few detailed patterns with instructions, it was limited to those few devotees who were able to draw patterns for themselves.

It is my pleasure, then, to offer you these new designs to bridge the gap and challenge your skills. You can use them in part or in whole as you wish.

You can also make your own variations such as the angle at which you place legs to make the character either run or stand still or how much you part the kookaburra's top and bottom beaks to make him laugh or not. Such slight adjustments do not affect the instructions. So it's up to you.

Once you start your imagination going, these designs may give that extra bit of inspiration and spur you on to create your own. If you start out with children's designs, remember that children can be very fussy. My son didn't like the aeroplane design on page 59 because I'd originally made it without a nose cone. But once I'd corrected that technical error, he was delighted with his aeroplane jumper and wore it even after he'd outgrown it.

With children's design, I always try to incorporate either red, yellow or orange because these colours lift everything out of the dull and drab. The dinosaur, for example, on page 46 would have been dreary if it didn't have the red and yellow of the sun and its rays to perk it up. I love designing for children because they react with such delight.

So use your appliqué to spread delight and delight yourself as well.

Happy stitching!

Jan Brooke

Front cover: Australian Native Animal Wall-hanging (see page 12).
Back cover: *left*, Lady's Face (see page 92); *right*, Australian Gumnuts (see page 85).

CONTENTS

PART ONE

GENERAL INSTRUCTION

EQUIPMENT FOR APPLIQUÉ

Sewing Machine

You can start with a basic sewing machine provided it will do a zigzag stitch that can be closed up to resemble a closely stitched buttonhole. Obviously, if you have a machine that will reduce an even-sided stitch, it will produce a more professional finish.

I set my **thread tension** at 3 as this enables me to use a **white bobbin** and it will not show through the top stitching. The usual thread tension on my machine is 5. If your machine does not have a numbered dial for thread tension start by adjusting it slightly lower than your usual tension.

I set the **stitch width** at 3 and the **stitch length** at 1/2. The only time I adjust the stitch width is when I am reducing, such as at the end of leaves or sewing very small circles. My machine reduces its stitch width evenly from both sides, but this is not the case in all machines, so please check your machine before starting.

Not all machines have stitch width or stitch length knobs. Try setting your machine stitch width at the second-last setting and move it backward and forward until you have a stitch width of approximately 3 mm.

For the stitch length, adjust it until you have a closed-up stitch (a satin stitch) but not so tightly that it prevents the machine from moving smoothly along the fabric.

It is advisable to have some sample pieces of fabric with your double-sided iron-on interlining pressed to the back and do some samples. Adjust it until you have a firm, even satin stitch that moves freely.

For best results, it is advisable to use an **embroidery foot** as this allows the stitching to rise up in a small mound giving a nice rounded shiny appearance. The standard sewing foot will press the stitching flat.

There is also an **appliqué foot** that is very good for doing circles as it has a rounded edge. I personally prefer to use my embroidery foot for my work, only using the appliqué foot for circles. I find the smaller appliqué foot is unable to rise up over previous stitches. Where you may have stitched down the side of a jumper and are now doing the stripes, the embroidery foot allows you to stitch right up to the previous stitching. The appliqué foot stops a little short leaving a very small gap.

If your machine has a **pressure dial** it should be set approximately halfway between what your usual setting is and what you would have it set at if you were using a very lightweight fabric.

If your machine has a **slow** button, it is useful when sewing circles and areas where you would normally slow down your sewing speed.

To secure the threads of your appliqué, do a small reverse stitch at either end and pull the remaining thread through to the back and tie it off. If your machine has an **auto-lock** use that as it places six very small stitches in the same hole and secures your thread. Check to see if your machine has an auto-lock button as it is a great time-saver and prevents unravelling.

Needles

The type of needle will largely depend on your machine. If unsure, refer to your machine dealer. I have used both Universal (woven fabric needles) and Ballpoint (stretch fabric needles). I found that the Ballpoint needle made a smoother incision into the material, whereas the Universal tended to make a small hole that weakened the appliquéd design and the backing fabric. Again, check this on your sample run.

For leather or suede work, you will need a 'wedge point leather needle' or the type specified by your machine manufacturer. It is important not to use your usual needle for suede or leather. The leather needle will puncture a hole first thus allowing the thread to flow through smoothly and avoiding skipped stitches.

You will also require a special Teflon leather foot, available from your machine dealer or sewing shop. This allows the leather or suede to glide freely.

Scissors

The type of scissors you have can make appliqué enjoyable or a chore. It is advisable to have your usual dressmaking scissors, an old pair for cutting paper and a small straight fine pointed pair, about 150 cms (6 in) long, plus a small strong curved nail sicssors, which I always keep on a piece of elastic and hang around my neck or on the door to the sewing room. That way I always know where they are. Mind you, it also means the other members of my family also always know where they are, but they know it means certain death to remove them without permission. Removing scissors from your sewing domain always causes a problem. I have solved that problem by providing a similar set of scissors for the other members of the family and put them in a place where they can always be found.

Having your small scissors on elastic allows you to extend to reach the far corners of your work.

Iron

You will need a good steam-and-dry iron. It will be necessary for you to have a good **pressing cloth** and a steam-and-dry **iron cleaner.** You will find that no matter how careful you are, you will always have some of your double-sided iron-on interlining come off onto your iron. This will leave a dirty mark on your design unless it is cleaned off. I prefer to place a piece of unwaxed greaseproof paper as a safeguard over my fabric whenever I am using the iron.

Miscellaneous Items

Dressmaker's carbon in light and dark colours is required to transfer lines, such as facial expressions on animals. You cut out a mirror-reverse pattern in your carbon, place it over the face and tape it into position so it will not move. Then, using either a dressmaker's **tracing wheel**, or a reasonably sharp pencil (not too sharp or it will tear the carbon) trace on the lines. (Ballpoint pens are too sharp.)

There are also **transfer pencil**s on the market. I have not had a lot of success with these as you have to have a very light colour for it to show up. I prefer to use either an **HB or 2B pencil**, directly on the fabric. If you haven't covered it up with your stitching, it will wash out easily. Beware of using anything that is permanent. It is always possible to make a mistake and it can spoil your whole design if you go over the line and *it will not wash out.*

For those who have trouble drawing, make a separate pattern from lightweight cardboard of the facial expressions such as the mouth of the koala. (See page 73) Cut the cardboard right up to the line leaving about 1.25 cm (1/2 in) below that so it is manageable and position the pattern where the line is to be drawn and trace the outline in pencil.

Place the top line level with the mouth and draw.

Keep in stock supplies of:
Double-sided iron-on interlining (Vliesofex)
Lightweight **cardboard**
Self-seal **plastic envelopes** for pattern pieces
Keep a pair of fine **tweezers** handy as it is invaluable for handling fiddly bits and pieces

COLOUR IN APPLIQUÉ

Colour is one of the most important aspects in appliqué design. Without strong, vibrant colours, your design becomes lifeless and this is why primary colours work so well.

That does not mean that you cannot use various types of design in the one colour such as black and white combinations of spots, stripes, and other patterns. Or you may wish to use Liberty-type prints of small flowers together with larger flowers, spots, and stripes.

In appliqué the usual principals of colour do not always apply. You may wish to use a strong hot pink with a vibrant orange and they could work well, or perhaps that same orange could be teamed up with a strong yellow and look equally effective. The colours you choose should be what you are happy with, not necessarily what should or should not go together. Be adventurous! Try colours you normally would not team together and you may be surprised to see how effective they can be.

When I am deciding what colours I will use, I place small samples of the colours onto the background colours. Sometimes the colours you think will work will alter the whole effect when placed on the background fabric. I generally tend to choose my colours and then pick up variations of those colours. Sometimes too many colours can spoil the effect.

When choosing the colours for the animals for the native animal wall hanging, I intended to use a pink and white cockatoo but upon placing those colours onto the design, it just didn't complement the other animals. I settled on the kookaburra in the browns and blues because it harmonised with the existing colours. The very colourful rosella and the yellow blossoms and the touch of orange and red was enough to brighten the overall picture.

Sometimes you may need to cut out your patterns in the colours you have chosen and place them onto the background. If the colours do not grab you immediately, you may need to rethink your colour scheme.

Choosing the colour scheme is a part of appliqué

design that needs time to be spent on it. It cannot be rushed.

In some cases I have spent up to three days trying different combinations for a design. I had used a dark brown for the gumnuts in the Australian gumnut design, making it dark and dull. I tried using red to brighten it up but that didn't work. I changed the gumnuts to avocado green and that didn't work. It wasn't until I used a cinnamon colour for the gumnuts and changed some of the leaves from green and khaki green to orange and differents shades of greens that it all worked. The overall effect was of blended colours but still bright and correct colours of the Australian bush.

On the whole, I try to use technically correct colours of Australia for wildlife designs, but for playful designs like the clowns and funny animals like the mouse, etc., you can use any combinations you wish.

FABRICS FOR APPLIQUÉ

The fabrics you choose for your design should always be closely woven and preferably strong, colourfast cottons.

The type of fabric largely depends on its function: whether it will be a wall hanging that you don't intend to wash or a garment that can only be dry-cleaned. For all designs that are to be washed, you must choose hard-wearing cottons and corduroys. Polyester satins can also be used as they wash well and give strong bright shiny effects. For designs that will not be washed regularly, you can experiment with leather, suede, or any of the metallic fabrics on the market.

On the native animal wall hanging I used a strong textured linen not normally recommended, because it is usually of a loose weave. They do not handle well and tend to fray. But because this one was tightly woven and because it was ironed onto the double-sided interlining it was able to be used without distortion.

There are many exciting fabrics to choose from, but remember that some may look exciting but may not always be suitable. Satins can be deceiving. One way to check on whether a satin will stand up to appliqué is to run your fingernail across the fabric and if it snags, it will not work. Another way is to press some sticky tape onto the correct side of the fabric and then pull it off. If the satin snags, it is not suitable.

If you have doubts about a certain fabric, take a small sample and test it by attaching it to a larger scrap and putting it into your washing machine and watch the results. If it fails in any way, treat it with caution unless you intend it to be used on a design that won't get such treatment.

LEATHER APPLIQUÉ

Leather or suede is a little more difficult to handle than cottons but gives such stunning effects that make it worth the extra effort.

As mentioned before, you will require a special needle and foot. (See page 4)

Always keep your shapes simple and not too small as leather does not swing under the foot as easily as cotton.

As the edges on leather or suede do not fray, you only need to sew in a straight stitch. For the more experienced you can satin stitch the edges but straight stitch your design first.

Do not pin or use sticky tape on your leather or suede. Pins will leave a permanent hole in your work and sticky tape will leave a residue on the surface. Use a special glue for leather and suede. Apply a small dab under the edges of the fabric and once it is dry, you can machine.

Do not begin sewing your leather or suede until you are completely happy with the layout of the design as once the leather or suede has been sewn, the needle leaves a permanent puncture in the fabric. If you do have to unpick your stitching, you will have to cut back where you have stitched.

If you follow these few simple hints you will have a trouble-free time.

DECORATION ON APPLIQUÉ

Sequins: A colourful and exciting way to decorate your appliqué. It is one of my favourites, even though they will not stand a lot of hard wear or washing. So, reserve them for garments that you will hand wash or dry-clean. When hand washing, gently wash the soiled areas first and then dunk the garment in a suitable washing solution. Do not use bleach of any kind or strong types of soaps. Do not apply soap of any kind directly to the sequins as it will take out all the colour. Although sequins require a little extra effort, the results are very striking. Another tip is to place the garment in a pillow-case and loosely stitch the opening. Wash in the machine on gentle.

Beads: Coloured glass beads can also create striking effects, but may require the same treatment as sequins. Wooden beads can take more wear and can be used for a variety of effects.

Diamanté: These also create an exciting effect on your appliqué and may be glued to the fabric. Check with your local handicraft store for the correct glue. You can also use a metal backing with claws that you push through the fabric and then close around the stone. These will take a little more wear and tear than sequins and can look great. Try them on your cat's bow tie, when next you do one.

Feathers: Combined with leather or satin can look very unusual. Where possible, I attach them with Velcro so they can be detached for washing or dry-cleaning.

Fabric Paint: Combined with your appliqué you can create special effects. If you prefer, you can paint the faces on your animals. Remember you must always set your paint with a hot iron.

EMBROIDERY ON APPLIQUÉ

Embroidery, either by hand or machine, can complement your designs and is especially helpful when an area is too small for you to machine successfully. It can be used to add texture, such as in the feathers of birds, etc.,

There will be times when it is advisable to hand-embroider rather than attempt to machine the parts of your design that are very small, such as the pupil of eyes on small animals. I have included some basic embroidery steps that you may find useful.

When hand-embroidering, leave a length of thread at the back and place two very small stitches into the back of the fabric, to prevent unravelling.

It is *not* advisable to knot your thread as it will form a small bulge that could show at the front of your design. You also run the risk of the knot unravelling at a later date.

Stem Stitch

A simple stitch for stems and lines. Used as a filling by working rows close together.

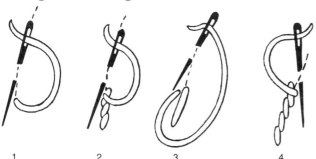

1. Bring the thread through material at lower end of line to be worked. Take even, slightly slanting stitches along the line to be worked.

2. Working from left to right, bring thread out on left of previous stitch.

Stem (extended)

3. The length of the stitch is doubled.

Stem (outline)

4. Suitable for working curved outlines. Work from left to right, and bring thread out on right of the previous stitches.

Satin Stitch

Suitable for working circles, leaves, petals, etc. Do not make stitches too long.

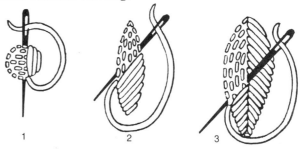

1. If desired, first pad with either running or chain stitch. Work the satin stitch evenly and close, in the opposite direction to the padding, keeping an even edge. Keep thread to right of needle.

Satin (sloped)

2. The satin stitch is at an angle to the running stitch.

Satin (divided)

3. Use where area to be worked is too wide for sloped satin. Mark a centre line and work two rows sloping in opposite directions.

Buttonhole Stitch

Used for finishing scalloped edges and outlining designs in Richelieu and cutwork.

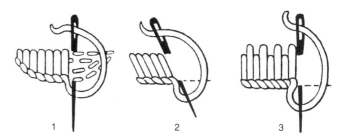

1. For scallops—place a fairly fine running stitch along outside edge, then pad centre with running stitch. Proceed with buttonhole stitch. Work from left to right, using thumb to keep thread under needle.

Buttonhole (sloping)

2. This is done the same as traditional buttonhole but the stitches are sloped to the right.

Buttonhole (long & short)

3. Each alternate stitch is shorter.

Running Stitch

1. Sew in and out of the material along the line to be worked, keeping stitches to an even length.

Running Stitch (overcast)

2. Using a contrasting thread, whip over each stitch—not through the fabric—making a continuous line.

Chain Stitch

Used for outlining or filling.

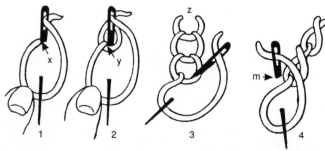

1. Bring thread up from under-side of material at (x), hold thread down with left thumb and insert needle at (x). Take small stitch to (y), pull needle through keeping thread below needle.

2. Continue by reinserting needle at (y).

Chain (open)

3. A space is left at (z).

Chain (twisted)

4. The needle is inserted outside preceding loop at (m).

French Knots

Bring needle through material at the spot required.

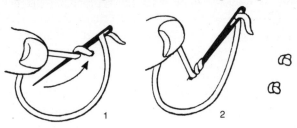

1. Twist needle around thread twice, hold tight with left thumb.

2. Turn needle back almost to starting point, and push through material.

Finish off if a single knot, or proceed to the next knot.

Cross Stitch

When working this stitch commence:

1. At bottom right and work to the left to end of the row.

2. Working from left to right, complete the cross. It is important that the upper halves of the cross all lie in the same direction.

Cross (double)

3. Double cross stitch consists of one complete cross worked over another.

APPLIQUÉ CIRCLES

Circles are one of the most difficult shapes to do with a professional finish. One slight movement and your circle will not be perfectly round. Here are a few points to help you get a professional finish:

1. Do not make your circles too small; the smaller the circumference, the tighter the turn of fabric. If you haven't attempted circles, try a few samples until you are satisfied with your finished product.

2. A paper backing will hold the fabric and you will find the whole article will swing in a smooth manner. Go slowly and steadily. If your machine has a slow button, use it when doing small circles.

3. Make sure you have no obstructions around your machine, such as cotton reels, pin cushions, etc. You need a completely clear area to swing your material around.

4. It is advisable to always work on the front of your garment before you sew it together. If you attempt to work on a completed garment, you will find the sleeves and sheer bulk will handicap you. If you must work on a completed garment, check to see if you can easily unpick at least one side. After a few unsatisfactory attempts to appliqué other people's completed garments, I made it a rule to always make the garments myself, thereby having the front to work on before it was completed.

5. In the case of the wall-hanging (see page 12) I placed the pygmy possum on another piece of unwaxed greasproof paper and stitched the eyes on before I pressed it to the background fabric. I then removed the unwaxed greaseproof paper and the protective paper backing of the interlining and pressed it to the wall-hanging. It was so much easier.

6. If it is your first attempt to appliqué circles, choose a child's garment to work on. That way, the actual piece of material you will be sewing on will be smaller and easier to handle.

7. If your machine has sewn (not you, of course) slightly crooked, go around once again, taking care when you reach the crooked part to make sure that the needle stays on the outside of the fabric circle. This should straighten the circle. Failing that and if it's very noticeable, it is advisable to unpick it by cutting the threads at the back and pulling the starting thread at the front. It should then unravel in one piece. Now reappliqué the circle.

8. Do not despair if you cannot make perfect circles all of the time. I still can't. Some days, you may not be able to sew a smooth circle for love or money. If that is the case, leave it and go and have a cup of something and come back to it later. Sometimes, the more you try the worse it gets, and it is most important that you enjoy what you are doing.

9. It is important to pivot regularly around the circle; the smaller the circle, the more you will need to pivot.

10. I also find that pressure on the forefinger and thumb moves the circle more freely. Apply more pressure to the forefinger than the thumb. That, and holding the backing paper and the material with your right hand, allows the circle to swing in a free manner.

HOW TO PIVOT

Before you start any appliqué work, do some samples of a pivot. It will make your work a lot easier. Instead of driving your material through the machine like you would drive a heavy truck, it will glide through effortlessly.

1. Outside Corner

Stitch to corner, leave needle in material. Pivot and continue stitching along the material edge.

2. Inside Corner

Stitch past the edge of the material the same distance as the stitch width. Pivot and continue stitching along material edge.

3. Outer Curve

Pivot on right-hand side of stitch. The size of circle will determine just how many times you will need to pivot.

4. Inner Curve

Pivot on right-hand side of stitch. The depth of curve will determine how many times you will need to pivot. In the case of water, you will need to pivot on the left-hand tip of each curve.

5. Outer Point

Stitch to (A) then gradually reduce stitch width to (0). Stitch just past point and pivot. Now, gradually increase stitch width back up to (3).

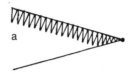

HELPFUL HINTS

Pre-wash any fabric that may run.

Place all your pattern pieces in plastic bags with a self-seal so they won't be lost.

Before construction, it is a help to place the original drawing beside you to work out the arrangement of the pattern pieces.

If you've pressed something to the fabric and then decide it should be moved, leave it for a day or so when it will start to lift so you can carefully pull it off.

By the same token, if you start your design construction and have steam pressed it to the background (but not yet stitched it) and have to leave it for a day or so, you will then need to press it down again with the steam iron to make sure it all thoroughly adheres.

In the process of construction, use your tweezers for fiddly bits and pieces as the fabric tends to stick to your fingers and moves as soon as you have placed it.

If double-sided iron-on interlining and wadding does not stick to the fleecy, do it in two sections or stitch a straight stitch around the material and wadding outline onto the fleecy. Then appliqué.

Always use unwaxed greaseproof paper behind your garment fabric as this stops the stretching that gives a puckered look.

Keep your sewing table clear of any obstructions. The slightest bump can cause a bump in your stitching.

If you intend to use coloured bobbins, have plenty of spare ones available. Fill these with the colours you will be using before you start.

Always sew so your needle is just outside the material thereby giving a clean neat edge at all times and avoiding loose threads.

Always sew in a smooth and steady manner, never in a stop-start fashion as it shows in your work.

Always have your stitch width closed up sufficiently to stop loose threads showing through.

When unpicking (and you should if it is not right), cut the threads at the back, turn it over and pull the starting thread. It should unravel. If not, carefully pull out the cut threads.

After completion of your appliqué design on woven fabric, give it a wash in cold water with a dash of salt. Let it drip dry until damp. Iron it on the wrong side and when almost dry, press on the correct side. This gives a beautifully pressed look to your work. You may find that some stretch fabrics can be pressed, but take care not to stretch the fabric.

Never appliqué when you are not in the mood as it will show in your work. Leave it for a time when you will enjoy what you are doing. It should be fun!

CONSTRUCTION TECHNIQUE

For detailed instructions on correct construction procedures see the colour photographs opposite page 17.

REDUCTION AND ENLARGEMENT OF DESIGNS

From time to time you will require designs in different sizes from those illustrated. The easiest way to reduce or enlarge a pattern is to use a photocopier with these facilities. However there is a simple method of altering the size of a drawing and still keep it in proportion.

First of all, draw in pencil a grid of squares over the design to be altered. Another grid is then drawn on a separate sheet of paper with larger or smaller squares depending on the alteration required. These would be calculated as near as possible to fractions of the original drawing squares.

For example:

Suppose your original pattern is drawn with a grid of 20 mm squares.

To **enlarge** your drawing by 25% you would need to draw the new grid with squares of 25 mm. That is 20 mm plus one-quarter of 20 mm (5 mm).

To **reduce** your drawing by 25% you would need to draw the new grid with squares of 15 mm. That is 20 mm less one-quarter of 20 mm (5 mm).

It is then a simple matter of copying that part of the drawing within each square. (See illustrations opposite).

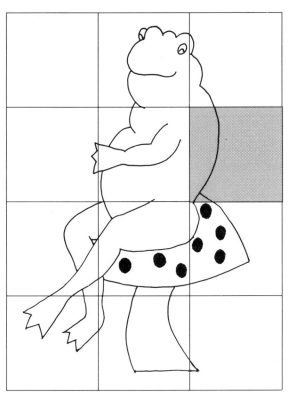

To enlarge pattern 25% draw
a 25mm grid

Actual size—20mm grid

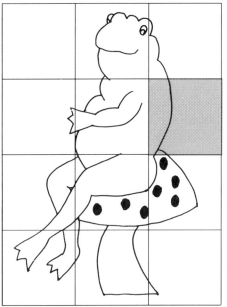

To reduce pattern 25% draw
a 15mm grid

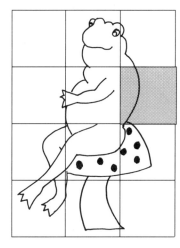

PART TWO

DESIGNS, PATTERNS AND INSTRUCTIONS

AUSTRALIAN NATIVE ANIMAL WALL-HANGING

This wall-hanging has been made from a series of individual designs. The final layout is left up to you. The pattern details have been reduced to 75%. See page 10 for instructions on enlarging them to full size.

PYGMY POSSUM

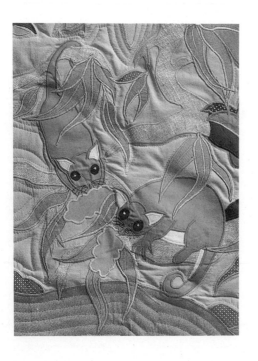

Pygmy Possum Master Design

Pygmy Possum Detail

body

body

blossom

blossom

tail

outer ear

belly

eyes

inner ear

Branches and Leaves Detail

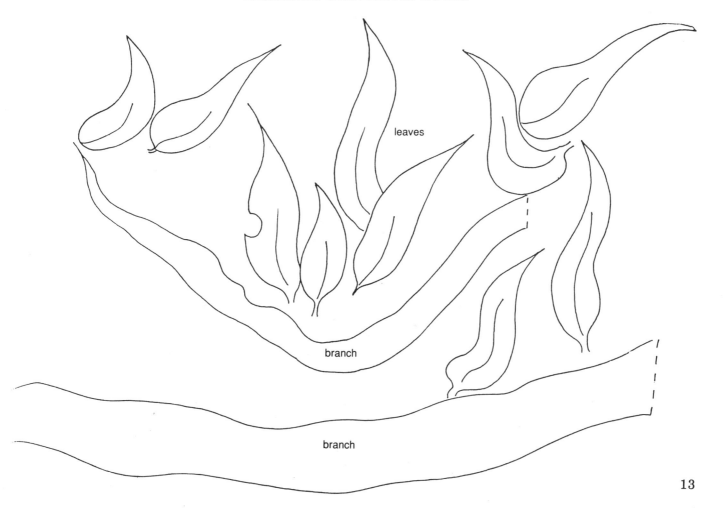

leaves

branch

branch

13

Materials Required

Fabric

Possum	32 x 32 cm	(13 x 13 in)
Leaves	20 x 16 cm	(8 x 6 in)
Branch	20 x 25 cm	(8 x 10 in)
Blossom	10 x 10 cm	(4 x 4 in)
Calico (belly)	6 x 6 cm	(3 x 3 in)
Eyes	4 x 4 cm	(2 x 2 in)

Pink cotton to lift the possum
Double-sided iron-on interlining
Dressmaker's carbon, tracing wheel
Unwaxed greaseproof paper
HB pencil
Cotton thread to match or highlight

Construction Procedure

Measure out required amounts of fabric. Mark out your pattern pieces and cut approximate squares of each colour.

Cut out similar squares of your double-sided iron-on interlining slightly smaller so it will not stick to your ironing board or iron.

Turn your fabric wrong side up and place your interlining over the material square, paper upwards, sticky side to the material, making sure there is no overhang to stick to the ironing board. Press with a dry iron.

Place your pattern pieces, mirror-reverse on to the paper backing and trace around your patterns. Now cut these out.

Using a hard surface and your HB pencil or dressmaker's carbon, trace the facial lines onto the possums. Mark where the eyes will go.

Because the eyes are small, I placed extra unwaxed greaseproof paper behind the possum to take the place of the background garment and stitched the eyes onto the possum before placing the possum onto the background fabric. This allows you to swing the small possum figure more easily. Also, if you make a mistake with the small possum eyes you can easily cut out a new possum and start again. For the centre of the eye, I held the fabric still and inserted approximately 4 to 5 stitches on top of each other and secured the thread.

Now, remove the protective paper backing from the branch and place it into position. Now take the paper backing from the possums and place them into position, sliding the tail of the possum around and under the tree.

Now, place the inner ears and belly, tail, etc. into position. Now, place the blossoms close to the nose of the larger possum and over the nose of the smaller possum. Now, place the leaves under the blossoms and over the possums, etc.

Making sure all backing is removed, place unwaxed greaseproof paper over the design and press with a steam iron in one downward motion. Hold, lift, and then repeat in same manner until the entire design is adhered to the background fabric.

Place unwaxed greaseproof paper behind your background fabric and prepare your machine for stitching.

Stitching Procedure

Using pink cotton to outline the possums, thread your machine and wind your bobbin unless you intend to use white bobbin for all colours. (If you set your tension at 3, the white will not show through.)

Starting at the right ear of the larger possum, secure thread and come up to the tip of the ear. Reduce your stitch width and pivot. Come down the ear increasing your width and down around the face. Stitch the left ear in the same manner. Secure thread at end of ear and do the top of the head.

Now, go to the back of the possum behind the left ear, secure thread and stitch around back and down around the tail. Pivot around the curve and reduce at tip. Pivot and come back up the tail until you reach the hind leg and secure thread.

Now, come down the hind leg and pivot around the paw and back up again. Secure thread and do the top line of the belly. Now, secure thread and come down the front leg, reducing at end of claw and pivot at top and bottom of each claw. Secure thread.

For the smaller possum, start on the face as for the larger possum. Then do the body outline, reducing at tip of tail.

For the noses, I reduced to approximately 1/2 to 1 (slightly wider than a straight stitch) and stitched a fine outline of the nose. For the tip of the nose, I secured thread and held the fabric steady and with a stitch width of 4 placed approximately 6 to 8 stitches very close together, some overlapping. Secure thread.

Change to cream cotton and do the inner ears in the same manner as the outer ears. Secure thread.

Now, do the bottom line of the belly. Secure thread and come down to the tail and finish that. Secure thread. For the whiskers, I used the same width as the bridge of nose and finished with uneven lengths. Secure thread. Change to the colour of the branch and complete that reducing at any limb that is on its own and not covered by a leaf. Secure thread.

Change to the colour of the blossoms and secure thread. These are tight curves so you will need to pivot regularly. Secure thread at ends.

Change to the colour of the leaves and secure thread. Reduce your stitch width at the tips of the leaves and do a centre line three-quarters of the way down the leaf. Reduce at its end. Secure thread.

KOOKABURRA

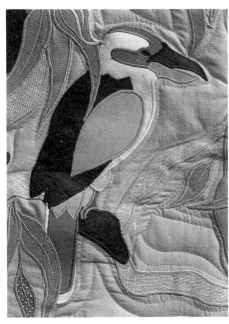

Kookaburra Master Design

Branches and Leaves Detail

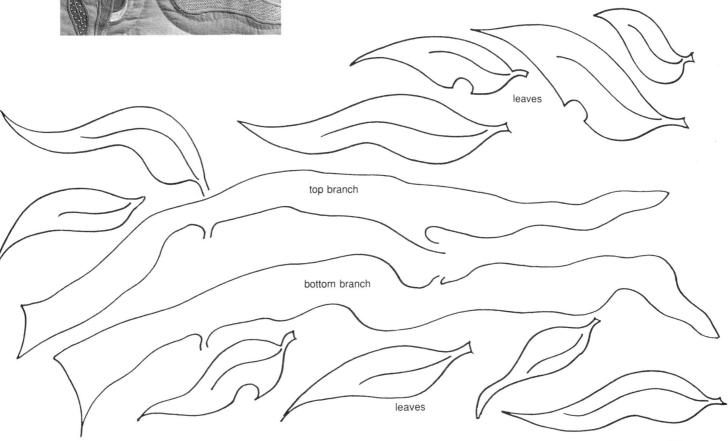

leaves

top branch

bottom branch

leaves

15

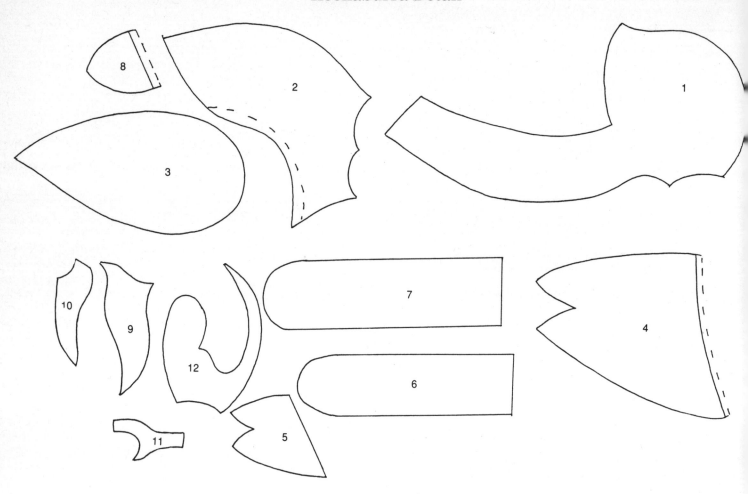

Materials Required

Fabric

Blue (3)	5 x 10 cm	(2 x 4 in)
Dark Brown (4)	7 x 7 cm	(3 x 3 in)
Calico (1) (8) (7)	10 x 14 cm	(4 x 6 in)
Choc Brown (2)	7 x 10 cm	(3 x 4 in)
Cinnamon (12) (6)	7 x 10 cm	(3 x 4 in)
Coffee (10)	2 x 5 cm	(1 x 2 in)
Grey (11)	2 x 5 cm	(1 x 2 in)
Branch	10 x 20 cm	(4 x 8 in)
Leaves	10 x 20 cm	(4 x 8 in)

Double-sided iron-on interlining
Dressmaker's carbon, tracing wheel
Unwaxed greaseproof paper
HB pencil
Cotton thread to match or highlight

Construction Procedure

Measure out required amounts of fabric. Mark out your pattern pieces and cut approximate squares of each colour.

Cut out similar squares of your double-sided iron-on interlining slightly smaller so it will not stick to your ironing board or iron.

Turn your fabric wrong side up and place your interlining over the material square, paper upwards, sticky side to the material, making sure there is no overhang to stick to the ironing board. Press with a dry iron.

Place your pattern pieces, mirror-reverse onto the paper backing, and trace around your patterns. Now cut these out.

Lay the head and breast (1) down first then lay the brown wing (2) overlapping the head. Then place the dark brown tail feathers (4) under (2). Then place the blue wing (3) over (2) and (4).

Then place the cinnamon (6) and calico (7) tail feathers under the right-hand peak of brown tail feathers.

Now, place the blue tail feathers (5) under the edge of the dark brown tail feathers (4) but over the tail feathers of (6) and (7).

Six Variations of Colour in One Design

Construction Technique

1. Measure out required amounts of fabric. Mark out your pattern pieces and cut approximate squares of each colour.

2. Cut out similar squares of your double-sided interlining. Always cut your interlining slightly smaller so it will not stick to your ironing board or iron.

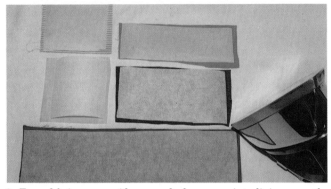

3. Turn fabric wrong side up and place your interlining over the material square, paper upwards, sticky side to the material, making sure there is no overhang to stick to the ironing board. Press with a **dry** iron.

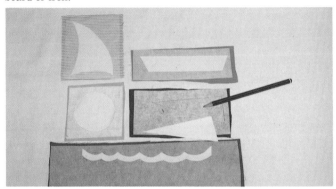

4. Place your pattern pieces, mirror-reverse onto the paper backing and trace around your patterns.

5. Now, cut out your pattern pieces. Using a hard surface and your pencil or dressmaker's carbon, trace out any facial features or extended lines of the design on the front side of the material.

6. Lay out your background fabric and proceed to assemble your design. Once you are satisfied with your layout, peel off, one at a time, the protective paper backing and replace onto the design.

7. Once you have reassembled the design, place unwaxed greaseproof paper over the design, and press with a **steam** iron. Do not slide the iron over the design until you are completely sure the design adheres firmly to the background.

8. Now, place unwaxed greaseproof paper behind your background fabric and prepare your machine for stitching. It is important to use unwaxed greaseproof paper or backing paper behind all designs as this prevents puckering and stretching.

Now, place the top part of the calico leg (8) under the calico breast (1) but over the grey claw (11).

Now, place the cinnamon head and eye (12) over the calico head (1) and place the top beak (9) over the edge of the cinnamon head (12) and partly over the bottom beak (10).

Now, place the bottom beak (10) under the top beak. The amount you part the beak depends on how much you want the kookaburra to laugh.

Now, slide the branch under the claw, and position the leaves. Once satisfied with the design, very gently, one by one remove the paper backing and replace into position. Once you have completed that, recheck the position and then place a piece of unwaxed greaseproof paper over the design.

Using a steam iron, hold it down over one section of the design. Lift and then hold down over the next section of the design. Continue in this fashion until the entire design has been completely adhered to the background fabric.

Place unwaxed greaseproof paper behind your background fabric and prepare your machine for stitching.

Stitching Procedure

Thread your machine with cream cotton to match the calico and wind your bobbin with the same colour, unless you intend to use white for all colours. (If you set your tension at 3, the white will not show through.)

Place your needle under the right-hand side (RHS) of the bottom beak, secure thread and come down around the breast to blend into the brown tail feathers. Insert your needle up close to that stitching for the calico leg. Secure thread and pivot where necessary. Come around until you meet the brown. Now, come down to the calico tail feathers and reduce your stitch width to blend in with the cinnamon tail feathers. Increase. Come around the tail feather and pivot at curve. Secure thread.

Now, with your design upside down, start on the back of the calico head nearest the brown wing. Secure thread and complete.

Change to cinnamon cotton and turn your design right way up. Secure thread, stitch the tail feathers and pivot at curve. Now, start at the cinnamon head nearest the bottom beak. Secure thread and come around the eye. Pivot regularly and across to the back of head. Pivot here and across top of head. Secure thread.

Change to dark brown cotton and place the needle right up against the cinnamon head top RHS. Secure

thread and come down across the top of the beak, reducing width at the tip of the beak. Pivot and come back across the beak, going slowly to get the right curves. Reduce width at corner and pivot, then increase width and stitch back to the start. Secure thread.

Now, go to the tail feathers and start at the RHS. Secure thread and reduce at peaks at top and bottom. Stitch back to the LHS.

Change to chocolate brown cotton and start at lower section near blue wing. Secure thread and come down to the peak. Reduce and then pivot and then increase as you come up to the back of the head. Pivot and come across the top, pivoting at the curve corners. Secure thread.

Change to blue and do the wing. Pivot at the top curve and reduce stitch width at the peak, secure thread. For the blue tail feathers, reduce your stitch width to start, secure thread and then increase. (That is so you can butt up right against the other stitching. You only need to do about 2 to 3 stitches reducing.) Stitch the blue tail feathers in the same manner as the others. Secure thread.

Change to coffee coloured thread for the lower beak and proceed in the same manner as for the top beak, but reduce for the first few stitches as for the blue tail.

Change to the colour to outline the branch. Secure thread and reduce at the ends of each branch. Secure thread each time you stop and finish.

Change to grey for the claw. Secure thread and start at the RHS under the calico leg and come down to the first claw. Reduce stitch width as you reach the branch and then increase it as you pivot around the curve. Stitch until you reach where the black section will start. Secure thread and start at the other side, working your way back to the LHS. Secure thread.

Change to black thread and set your stitch width so it will be same width as the grey and quickly reduce it right down to 0. Secure thread at start and finish.

For the eye, I started at 0 and quickly increased to 3 in the middle and back down again. You may, if you wish, use a hand-embroidered satin stitch.

Lastly, change the thread to the colour of your leaves. If you have green leaves, try using a sea green colour for a contrast. For the centre line, reduce your stitch width down to 0 at the end. Secure thread.

KOALA

Koala Master Design

Materials Required

Fabric

Grey	25 x 30 cm	(8 x 12 in)
Contrast spot	6 x 13 cm	(3 x 5 in)
Black	3 x 4 cm	(1 x 2 in)
White	12 x 12 cm	(5 x 5 in)
Tree trunk	35 x 40 cm	(14 x 16 in)
Leaves	10 x 20 cm	(4 x 8 in)
Contrast for bark	10 x 20 cm	(4 x 8 in)

Double-sided iron-on interlining
Dressmaker's carbon, tracing wheel
Unwaxed greaseproof paper
HB pencil
Cotton thread to match or highlight

Construction Procedure

Measure out required amounts of fabric. Mark out your pattern pieces and cut approximate squares of each colour.

Cut out similar squares of your double-sided iron-on interlining slightly smaller so it will not stick to your ironing board or iron.

Turn your fabric wrong side up and place your interlining over the material square, paper upwards, sticky side to the material, making sure there is no overhang to stick to the ironing board. Press with a dry iron.

Place your pattern pieces, mirror-reverse onto the paper backing and trace around your patterns. Now, cut these out.

Using a hard surface and your HB pencil or dressmaker's carbon, trace around the extended lines of the koala's legs, arms, etc. Mark in the facial lines and place a small mark where the top of the nose will go and the position of the eyes.

When laying out your design place your koala snuggling into the V of the tree trunk, with lots of leaves around him. The koala is not the prettiest of animals and does not have a lot of features to his face. Putting leaves all round him, as in his natural habitat helps to soften the design.

Now, place the main part of the body over the base of the tree to ascertain the position of the design. Remove the paper backing from the tree base and reposition. Place the koala body down into the V of the trunk then remove the paper backing. Place the top part of the tree under the koala in the same manner.

Koala Detail

chest

arm fits over this section

rear foot

mouth

nose

eye

arm

leaves

body

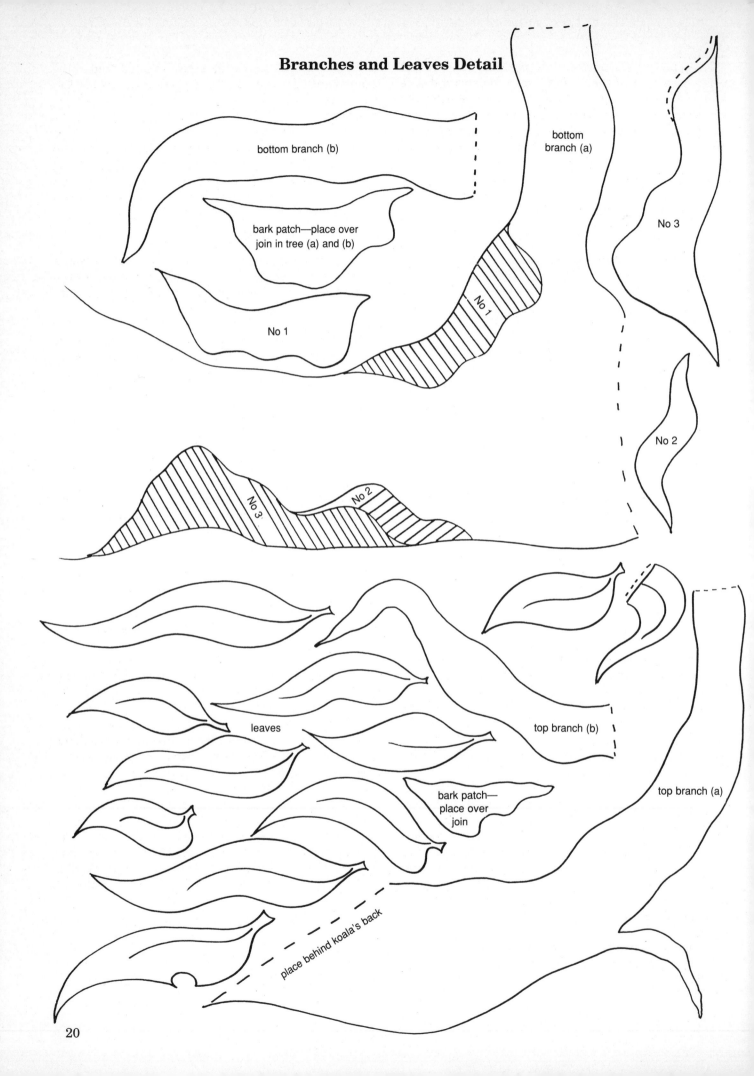

Branches and Leaves Detail

bottom branch (b)

bark patch—place over
join in tree (a) and (b)

No 1

No 1

bottom
branch (a)

No 3

No 2

No 3

No 2

leaves

top branch (b)

bark patch—
place over
join

top branch (a)

place behind koala's back

20

Now, place bark patches into position. Remove the paper backing from the koala's arms and paws and slide under the body. Now, remove the backing from the white fur and slide it under the grey body. Remove the backing from the head and place it down over the white section. Now, place any leaves that you are placing behind the koala's head.

After you are satisfied with the layout of the design, place unwaxed greaseproof paper over this part of the design and press with a steam iron. Hold iron in one movement down onto the design, repeat this motion until the entire design is completely adhered to the background fabric.

Now, take the pink mouth and the two leaves and trim the curved sections while you have the paper backing on, to fit into the mouth line.

Now, remove the backing and place into position. Do the same for the nose and eyes. Now press with your steam iron as before.

Arrange your leaves around and in some cases over the koala. He should look as though he is high up in the gum tree among the leaves. Steam press these as before.

Place unwaxed greaseproof paper behind your background fabric and prepare your machine for stitching.

Stitching Procedure

Thread your machine with the tree colour and wind your bobbin with the same colour, unless you intend to use white for all colours. (If you set your tension at 3, the white will not show through.)

Starting just below the grey body on the right-hand side (RHS), secure thread and come down that side to the base of tree. Pivot and come across the base and back up the other side, stopping to secure thread for each bark colour. Reduce stitch width down to 0 for all branches. Continue around the branches until complete. Change thread and do each bark section. Secure thread at start and finish.

Now change to grey cotton for the body of the koala. Start at the RHS of the koala under the white fur. Come down and around until you reach the hind leg. Secure thread and start at the top of the hind leg. Secure thread and come down around the hind leg, pivot at curves and reduce your stitch width at the tip of paws. Come around the curve and pivot at the end of paw. Stitch up to the arm and secure thread.

Now, move over to the extended line of the rear hind leg and do that next. Secure your thread at the start and finish.

Now, start at the arm, secure thread and come around until you join up with the leaves. Secure thread. Complete the top of the arm. Now finish the other arm and secure thread.

For the head, I usually start in the middle of the top of the head. Secure thread and pivot at curves. Reduce at each peak and reduce at the inside peak, pivot and continue in the same manner right around the head and ears. Secure thread.

Change to white and start just under the head, secure thread and come down the white section in the same manner as you have done the ears. Secure thread and go to the small section between the arms and paws. Secure thread at start and finish.

Now, change back to grey for the facial lines. Start with the mouth first. Secure thread and stitch slowly over the pink and green of leaves. Use your slow button if you have one. You may need to do this twice.

Now, do the cheek. Secure thread and follow your pencil line exactly and pivot regularly.

Now, change to pink cotton and do the mouth. Again, take it slowly and secure at each stop. Now change to brown and do the eyes. Reduce your stitch width right down and secure thread. Increase your width back up to 3 at the middle, and then back down again to 0 at the corner. Pivot and repeat the same for the bottom line and the other eye.

Change to black and set your width on 3. Insert your needle just under the brown stitching and finish just inside the lower brown stitching. Do not go over the brown stitching at all. Secure thread.

For the nose, do the nostrils first in a figure 8. Start at the middle of the top of the right nostril and come down to the middle and bottom line of the left side and around until you reach your start. Secure thread. Now, complete the remainder of nose. Secure thread and stitch up close to the figure 8 stitching, but not over it. Secure thread.

Now complete the design by doing the leaves. Try using a sea green cotton on some of the green leaves to give depth. Reduce your stitch width at the tips of the leaves and do a centre line in about a half of the leaves, reducing the stitch width at the end of the line. Do not take the line right down to the tip but about three-quarters of the way.

RAINBOW LORIKEET

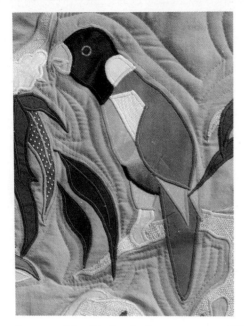

The branches used for the kookaburra on page 15 can be used for the lorikeet. Mirror reverse before tracing.

Rainbow Lorikeet Master Design

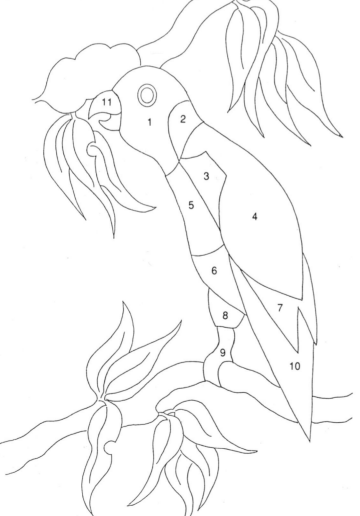

leaves

blossom

Materials Required

Fabric

Lime green (4) (10)	7 x 20 cm	(3 x 8 in)
Blue (1)	7 x 7 cm	(3 x 3 in)
Hot pink (7) (8)	4 x 6 cm	(2 x 3 in)
Gold (3) (9)	9 x 8 cm	(3 x 3 in)
Yellow (2)	3 x 3 cm	(1 x 1 in)
Red (5)	3 x 6 cm	(1 x 3 in)
Orange (11)	3 x 3 cm	(1 x 1 in)
Branch	10 x 20 cm	(4 x 8 in)
Leaves	10 x 20 cm	(4 x 8 in)
Purple (6)	4 x 5 cm	(2 x 2 in)

Blossoms included in gold

Double-sided iron-on interlining
Dressmaker's carbon, tracing wheel
Unwaxed greaseproof paper
HB pencil
Cotton thread to match or highlight

Construction Procedure

Measure out required amounts of fabric. Mark out your pattern pieces and cut approximate squares of each colour.

Cut out similar squares of your double-sided iron-on interlining slightly smaller so it will not stick to your ironing board or iron.

Turn your fabric wrong side up and place your interlining over the material square, paper upwards, sticky side to the material, making sure there is no overhang to stick to the ironing board. Press with a dry iron.

Place your pattern pieces, mirror-reverse onto the paper backing, and trace around your patterns. Now cut these out. Then using a hard surface, mark in the eye position.

Place the bottom branch into position to ascertain the layout for the design. Now remove the paper backing from the branch and place onto background fabric.

Now, remove the backing from the blue head (1) and place it into position. Then, remove the backing from the red breast (5) and place it under the blue head. Remove the backing from the purple section (6) and place it under the red breast. Now, place the hot pink leg (8) under the purple section. Place the gold claw (9) under the hot pink leg (8) so it sits on the branch with the bottom of the claw resting on the bottom line of the branch.

Now, place the green top wing (4) over the blue head and red breast. Slide the hot pink tail feathers (7) under

the top green wing (4) and the green tail feathers (10) under the hot pink tail feathers (7).

Now, place the gold wing section (3) on the edge of the green top wing (4) nearest the red breast (5) and just touching (1) and yellow back neck (2) and over the blue head (1) and just on the green line of (4). Now place the beak into position just over the blue head.

Remove the paper backing from the top branch and place it above the lorikeet's head. Now place the blossoms just above the beak. Now place the leaves around the design.

Check that nothing has moved and place a piece of unwaxed greaseproof paper over the design. Using a steam iron, press down over one part of the design, hold and lift. Then press down onto another section of the design. Repeat in this fashion until you have completely adhered the design to the background fabric.

Place unwaxed greaseproof paper behind your background fabric and prepare your machine for stitching.

Stitching Procedure

Thread your machine with blue cotton and wind your bobbin in the same colour, unless you intend to use white for all colours. (If you set your tension at 3, the white will not show through.)

Start nearest to the yellow section. Secure thread and come around to the orange beak, pivot at corner, and secure thread. Start at the top of the beak and secure thread and come around the top of the head. Secure thread. I have also outlined the purple section in blue to give balance.

Start at the green tail feathers, secure thread and finish at the red breast. Do not come across the breast. Change to red and start at the green feathers and come across to the corner. Pivot and come up the breast finishing at the blue stitching. Secure thread.

Change to hot pink and do the three sides of the leg. Secure thread and start at the inside and come down to the claw. Pivot, come across, pivot and back up to join the purple section.

For the tail feathers, start at the top right-hand side (RHS) nearest the green feathers. Secure and come down reducing at peaks and back to the left-hand side (LHS) side of the green tail feathers. Do not go across the green feathers. Secure thread.

Change to gold and do the three sides of the gold wing section (3) starting at the bottom of (3) nearest the curved line of the green feathers. Come up towards the head, pivot and come across to the next corner, pivot and go back down to the curved section of the green top wing.

Now, go to the claw. Start on the inside nearest the hot pink leg. Secure thread, pivot at the corners and come back up to the LHS of the leg.

Change to yellow for section (2) where you do all four sides. Secure thread at start and finish.

If your blossoms are yellow or gold now is the time to do them. Secure thread, and put your slow button on (if you have one) and take the curves carefully. Pivot where necessary and at the end of each curve and secure.

Change to orange for the beak and, starting at the top RHS of the bottom beak, come around the curve and reduce at the tip and pivot. Then pivot very carefully around the next section. Stop at centre line. Secure thread. Starting at centre line, secure thread and come around the curves. Reduce at tip of beak to the end of top beak. Secure thread.

Change to lime green thread and start at the RHS of the top wing under (2). Come down the back reducing your stitch width at the peak, pivot and come back up the other side, extending the curved section to cover the yellow of section (3). Secure thread.

Now, move to the green tail feathers. Secure thread and start right under the pink stitching. Come down the straight edge reducing your stitch width at the peak. Pivot and come back up the other side. Reduce your width as you blend into the other stitching. Secure thread.

Now, change your cotton to the colour of the branch. Start on the bottom right-hand side (RHS) of the branch. Stopping at either side of the tail feathers and secure the thread. Repeat for the claw and any leaves. Reduce your stitch width at the tip of the branch and come back up the other side. If you are including a top branch approach in same manner.

Now, change your cotton to the colours of your leaves and secure thread at start and reduce your stitch width as you come to the tip. Pivot and come back up the other side. For the centre line reduce your stitch width about halfway down. Only do this line about three-quarters of the way down the leaf and only do about half of the leaves.

The eye of the lorikeet is a black pupil surrounded by a thin red circle. I have on my machine a device that stitches in a circle, and used it for this design. For those who do not have a similar stitch, use a small stem stitch and hand-embroider. I didn't worry about the black pupil, as it is on the blue.

PLATYPUS

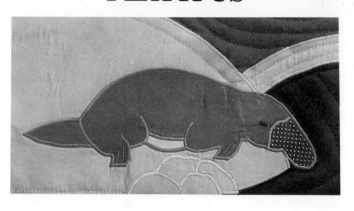

Materials Required

Fabric

Water	28 x 40 cm	(11 x 16 in)
Platypus, tree	16 x 27 cm	(6 x 11 in)
Bank	20 x 22 cm	(8 x 9 in)
Rocks	7 x 19 cm	(3 x 8 in)
Grass, tree	16 x 24 cm	(6 x 10 in)
Contrast grass	6 x 6 cm	(3 x 3 in)
Bill	5 x 6 cm	(2 x 3 in)
Rocks, belly	10 x 10 cm	(4 x 4 in)

Double-sided iron-on interlining
Dressmaker's carbon, tracing wheel
Unwaxed greaseproof paper
HB pencil
Cotton thread to match or highlight

Platypus Master Design

Platypus Detail

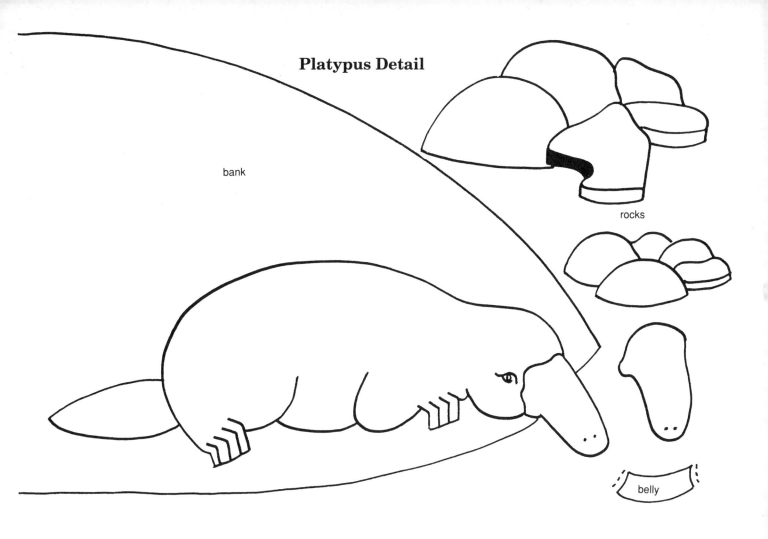

bank

rocks

belly

Grass Detail

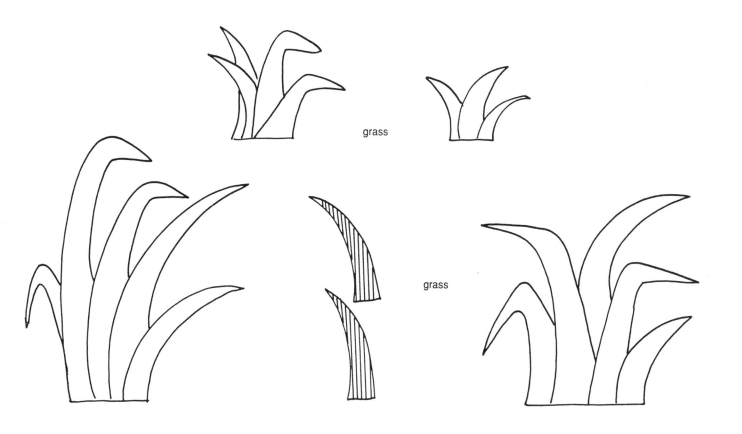

grass

grass

25

Pond and Tree Detail

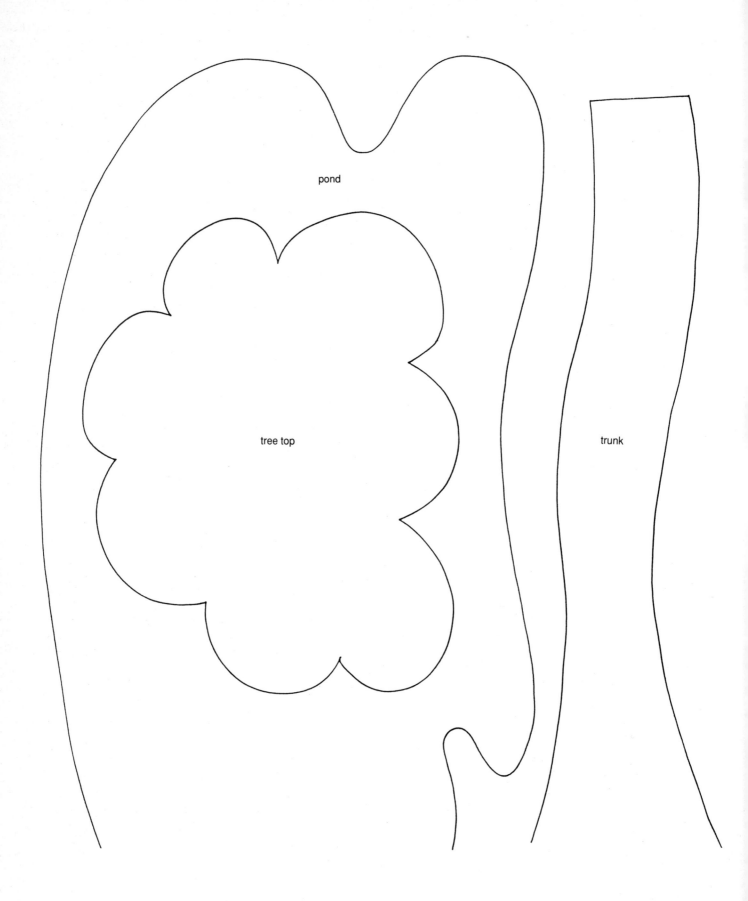

pond

tree top

trunk

Construction Procedure

Measure out required amounts of fabric. Mark out your pattern pieces and cut approximate squares of each colour.

Cut out similar squares of your double-sided iron-on interlining slightly smaller so it will not stick to your ironing board or iron.

Turn your fabric wrong side up and place your interlining over the material square, paper upwards, sticky side to the material, making sure there is no overhang to stick to the ironing board. Press with a dry iron.

Place your pattern pieces, mirror-reverse onto the paper backing, and trace around your patterns. Now, cut these out.

Using a hard surface and your HB pencil or dressmaker's carbon, trace the extended lines of the platypus and the rocks.

Lay your garment front on a large flat surface such as the floor and peel off the protective paper backing from the water. Place it into position. Now, lay the bank into position with the tree trunk over the straight edge of the bank. Peel off the paper backing from the platypus and place it so it sits on the bank with its head just touching the water. Now, place the bill over the head of the platypus and slide the belly under the body. Now, place the rocks into position and tufts of grass around it and on the bank.

Once you have the design as you want it, place unwaxed greaseproof paper over the design and leaving it where it is, bring the iron to it. Steam press each section of the design. Do not slide the iron over the design until you have completely adhered the design to the background fabric.

Place unwaxed greaseproof paper behind your background fabric and prepare your machine for stitching.

Stitching Procedure

Thread your machine with the colour you have chosen for the platypus and wind the bobbin the same colour, unless you intend to use a white bobbin for all colours. (If you set your tension at 3, the white will not show through.)

Set your stitch width at 3 1/4 and start at the left-hand side (LHS) of the back web foot of the platypus. Secure thread and stitch around the back of the platy-

pus until you reach the bill. Secure thread and come around to the other side of the bill. Start at the bottom of the bill and come around the curve and secure thread.

Now, butt right up to that stitching and do the small section between the curve of the chin and the front web. Secure thread and start on the front web. Pivot at corners and come up the other side. Pivot and come across the front leg, secure thread. Now, stitch the bottom line of the belly and secure thread at start and finish. Also do the top line of the belly in the same manner.

Go to the curve of the hind leg, secure thread and stitch until it joins up with the back web. Secure thread and start on the web coming down to the corner. Pivot and come across the bottom of the web, pivot and come back up the side to join up with your stitching. Now, secure thread at start of tail and reduce stitch width at tip of tail. Secure thread at finish. Reduce your stitch width to 1 or less for the internal lines of the web.

Now, change to black for the eye. I reduced the stitch width right down to 0. Secure thread and quickly increase the width to 3 and back down. You do not have much room to go up and down so you will need to reduce each stitch or so. For those who wish to hand-embroider, use a satin stitch.

Change to blue for the water and complete that. Now, change to the colour of the tree trunk and secure thread and start on the right-hand side (RHS) of the trunk coming down to the bank. Secure thread and go to the other side. Secure thread and go back up to the tree top.

Change to green and start on the tree top. Pivot regularly around the curves and secure thread at end.

To give contrast to the grass, choose a different colour for some of the grass and place it behind the brighter colour, such as khaki behind bottle green. Now, stitch the brighter grass first. Secure at the base of the grass and reduce at each tip and back down to the base. Continue in this way until complete. Come across the base and secure thread. Change to the background colour of the grass and continue in the same manner.

Change thread to contrast with the rocks and secure thread. Follow the pencil lines of the rocks. Secure thread.

Change to the colour of the bill and secure thread and follow the line of the bill from RHS to meet up again with the start of your stitching.

GIRL'S QUILT

This quilt has been made from a series of individual designs. The final layout of the quilt is left up to you. The designs can be used individually on sweatshirts, childrens' clothes or any item you like.

The pattern details have been reduced to 75%. See page 10 for instructions on enlarging them to full size.

CLOWN FACE

Clown Face Master Design

Materials Required

Fabric

Quilt square	30 x 36 cm	(12 x 14 in)
Mouth and eyes	9 x 10 cm	(4 x 4 in)
Flower (1)	10 x 10 cm	(4 x 4 in)
Flower (2)	10 x 10 cm	(4 x 4 in)
Hair	10 x 16 cm	(4 x 6 in)
Hat	11 x 14 cm	(5 x 6 in)
Face	17 x 22 cm	(7 x 9 in)
Collar	24 x 40 cm	(10 x 16 in)
Hat band	1 x 9 cm	(1/2 x 4 in)

Scrap of black for pupil and tears
Scrap of red for nose and cheeks
Coloured ribbons for collar   70 cm   (30 in) each
Sequins for flowers, hat and band if required
Double-sided iron-on interlining
Dressmaker's carbon, tracing wheel
Unwaxed greaseproof paper
HB pencil
Cotton thread to match or highlight

Hat, Hair and Flower Detail

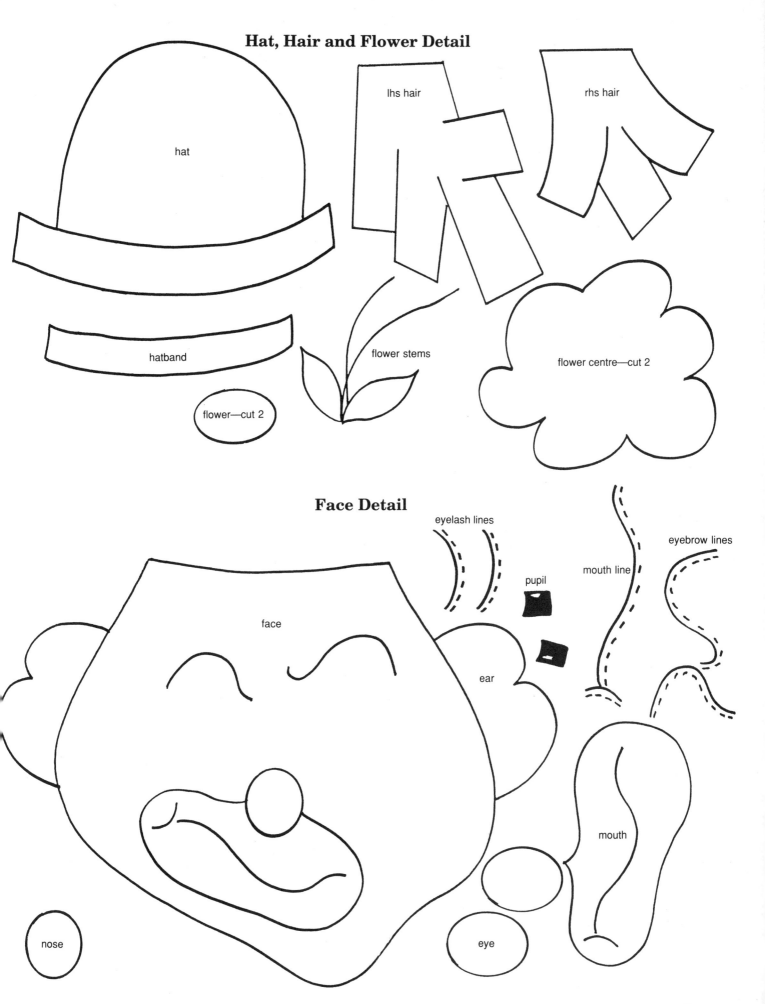

hat

lhs hair

rhs hair

hatband

flower stems

flower centre—cut 2

flower—cut 2

Face Detail

eyelash lines

eyebrow lines

pupil

mouth line

face

ear

mouth

nose

eye

Construction Procedure

Measure out required amounts of fabric. Mark out your pattern pieces and cut approximate squares of each colour.

Cut out similar squares of your double-sided iron-on interlining slightly smaller so it will not stick to your ironing board or iron.

Turn your fabric wrong side up and place your interlining over the material square, paper upwards, sticky side to the material, making sure there is no overhang to stick to the ironing board. Press with a dry iron.

Place your pattern pieces, mirror-reverse onto the paper backing, and trace around your patterns. Now, cut these out.

Sew a small hem on three sides of the collar. Sew on the ribbons with a small zigzag stitch. When complete, place on garment front under the face. Pin in the pleats and the two sides of the collar.

Remove the protective paper backing from the face and place it over the collar, leaving the pins in position. Steam press. Position hair and hat and remove paper backing and press.

Do not allow the iron to slide. Lift iron and hold it down until the design completely adheres to the background.

Place hatband into position with the leaves placed over the hatband. Now position flowers. Place yellow flower under the purple flower and place centres. Press with steam iron.

Cut out an identical face from your dressmaker's carbon but mirror reverse it, as the carbon side will face over the material face. Place pattern over the material and carbon face and, using a pencil, trace out the eyebrows. For those who can draw, simply draw them in with an HB pencil. For the eyes, nose and mouth just put a very small light mark inside the eye outline so that you will be able to line up the facial features.

Now, position the eyes, mouth, and nose. When happy with the position, carefully steam press them into place. Press the teardrops into position. The black pupils are small and fiddly so leave the protective backing on until you have made any necessary adjustments such as cutting in a small curve at the top to fit into the curve of the eyelashes. When satisfied, remove paper backing and steam press as before.

Using an HB pencil, lightly draw in the eyelashes. Cut out a mouth in dressmaker's carbon and, as you did for the face, trace out the mouth expression. When tracing over carbon on faces it is preferable to use a pencil rather than a tracing wheel, as you can get the free flow line with a pencil. Lastly, trace the cheek outline.

Place unwaxed greaseproof paper behind your background fabric and prepare your machine for stitching.

Stitching Procedure

Thread your machine with pink and wind your bobbin with the same colour unless you intend to use a white bobbin for all colours. (If you set your tension at 3, the white will not show through.)

Start on the right ear. Secure thread and stitch around the face finishing at the left ear. Now change to orange for the hair, remembering to extend the lines up past the cuts. Now change to green for the hatband and leaves. Only stitch the top and bottom of the hatband not the sides. You will cover them when stitching the sides of the hat. For the leaves, reduce at each tip and secure at finish. Place a folded piece of single-sided interlining behind the area you intend to stitch the stems of the flowers. Stitch them twice for better coverage.

Change to matching colour of hat and stitch the sides of the crown first. Secure thread and then stitch all four sides of the brim. If you intend to sequin later it is advisable to use the matching colour of the sequins not the fabric. Now, complete each flower and centres. Now, change to red thread for the nose and the cheeks. Pivot regularly around the nose and cheeks and secure the thread.

Change to black for the eyes. Stitch around the eyes first, pivot where necessary. Now, stitch the pupils, only do three sides, leave the top. Now stitch the eyelashes. Take care and follow your pencil lines exactly. If you do not achieve a curve, it is advisable to redo. Now, stitch the mouth, again take care to follow the pencil lines exactly. Finish by stitching the teardrops if you have included them in your design.

Change to white thread and stitch down the two edges of the collar, directly under the right and left hair. Do not stitch down the curved edge of the collar to which you have stitched ribbons. This allows it to float freely.

FROG ON TOADSTOOL

Materials Required

Fabric

Quilt square	30 x 36 cm	(12 x 14 in)
Frog	20 x 35 cm	(8 x 14 in)
Toadstool	20 x 24 cm	(8 x 10 in)
Stems	12 x 20 cm	(5 x 8 in)
White	8 x 8 cm	(3 x 3 in)
Black	4 x 4 cm	(2 x 2 in)

Double-sided iron-on interlining
Dressmaker's carbon, tracing wheel
Unwaxed greaseproof paper
HB pencil
Cotton thread to match or highlight

Toadstool and Eye Detail

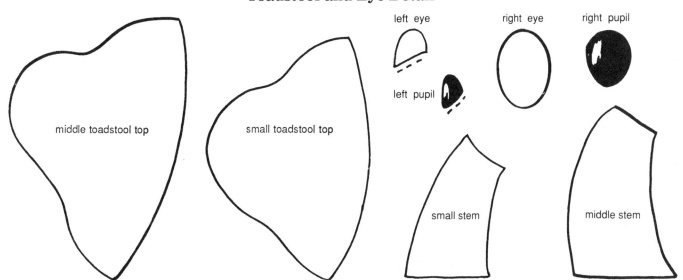

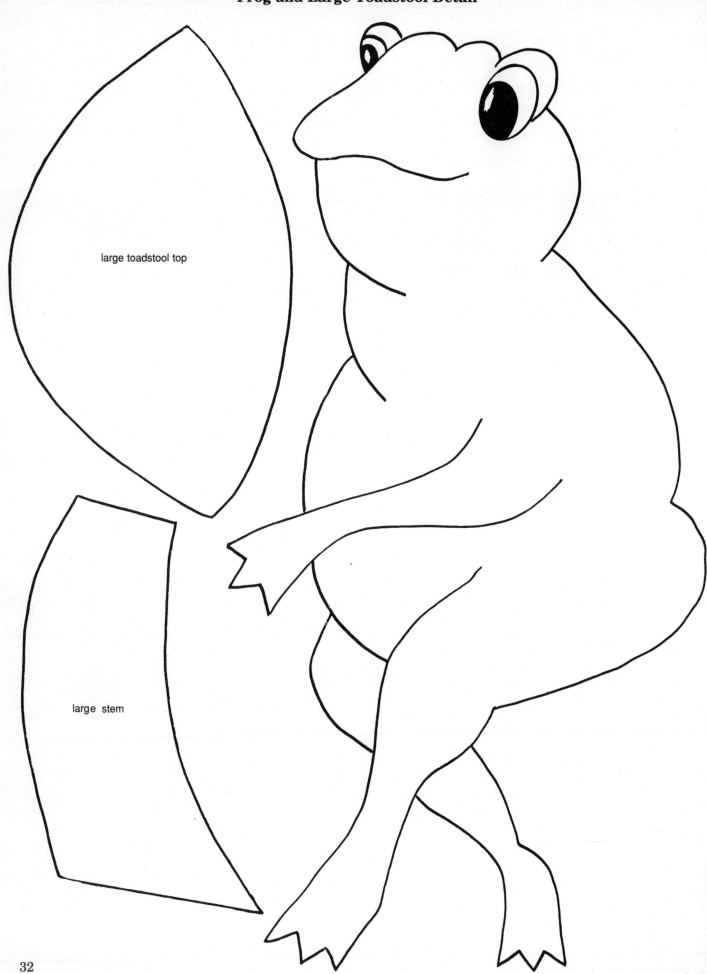

large toadstool top

large stem

Australian Native Animal Wall-hanging (see page 12).

Girl's Quilt (see page 28).

Construction Procedure

Measure out required amounts of fabric. Mark out your pattern pieces and cut approximate squares of each colour.

Cut out similar squares of your double-sided iron-on interlining slightly smaller so it will not stick to your ironing board or iron.

Turn your fabric wrong side up and place your interlining over the material square, paper upwards, sticky side to the material, making sure there is no overhang to stick to the ironing board. Press with a dry iron.

Place your pattern pieces, mirror-reverse onto the paper backing, and trace around your patterns. Now cut these out.

Using a hard surface and your HB pencil or dressmaker's carbon, trace the extended lines on the frog. Make a small mark where the eyes will go.

Peel off the paper backing from the body of the frog and place into position. Then take the backing from the large toadstool and slide it under the frog. Then remove the backing from the other toadstools and place into position. Now, remove the paper backing from the stems and slide them under the toadstools. If using a lighter material for the tops of the toadstools, trim the darker stems so they will not show through the lighter material. Leave just enough for the stitching to cover.

Now remove the backing from the left eye and place it under the face of the frog. Then slide the white over that but under the face and slide under the black pupil in the same manner. Now, place the white eye of the right-hand side (RHS) into position and the black pupil so it just sits on the outer line of the white eye.

Press with a steam iron but do not allow the iron to slide. Lift iron and hold down until all sections of the design adhere to the background fabric.

Place unwaxed greaseproof paper behind your background fabric and prepare your machine for stitching.

Stitching Procedure

Thread your machine with bright lime green cotton, and wind your bobbin with the same colour, unless you intend to use a white bobbin for all colours. (If you set your tension at 3, the white will not show through.)

Set your stitch width at 3 and start at the right-hand side (RHS) just under the eye. Secure thread and stitch down and around the back of the frog. Stitch until you come to the web of the foot. Reduce your stitch width at the tip, pivot and then increase the stitch back up, and down again as you reach the inside peak. Pivot and repeat each one in the same manner.

Note: If your machine does not reduce stitch width, stitch right to the corner of webb and pivot. Come across in a squared corner.

Come up that leg and stop. Secure thread and come around to the leg that sits under that one. Secure thread and stitch that leg in the same manner as the other leg. Secure thread and come across to the other side of that leg. Secure thread and stitch to the belly. Secure thread and stitch the belly, stopping at each side of the arm and secure thread. Stop at the double chin. Secure thread and do each curve separately. Secure thread at each end.

Now start on the mouth. Start from the inside under the eye and stitch to the corner. Pivot and make a definite turn and then come back up around the head to the start and secure thread. Now, finish the left eye. Pivot regularly and go to the arm, which you stitch in the same manner as the legs. Secure threads.

Change to the colour of the large toadstool. Start at the right-hand side (RHS) under the frog and stitch down to the corner. Pivot and stop and secure each side of the leg. Pivot at corner and secure thread at end. Change to the colour of the smaller toadstools and complete those.

Change to white and complete the stems of the toadstools. How, go to the eyes and complete them, and lastly the pupils.

BUTTERFLY

Butterfly Master Design

Wing Detail

middle wing section

bottom wing section

Body and Branch Detail

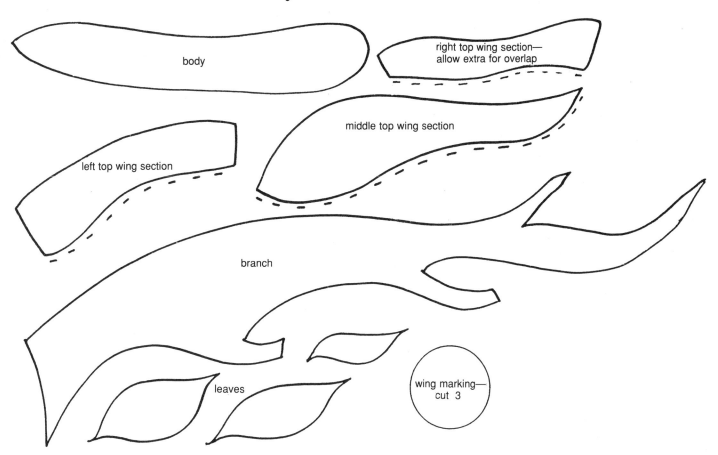

Materials Required

Fabric

Quilt square	30 x 36 cm	(12 x 14 in)
Body (green)	3 x 16 cm	(2 x 7 in)
Bottom wing	11 x 30 cm	(4 x 12 in)
Middle wing	10 x 32 cm	(4 x 13 in)
Top wing	6 x 31 cm	(3 x 12 in)
Branch	8 x 16 cm	(3 x 16 in)

Scraps of blue and green for leaves

Double-sided iron-on interlining
Dressmaker's carbon, tracing wheel
Unwaxed greaseproof paper
HB pencil
Cotton thread to match or highlight

Construction Procedure

Measure out required amounts of fabric. Mark out your pattern pieces and cut approximate squares of each colour.

Cut out similar squares of your double-sided iron-on interlining slightly smaller so it will not stick to your ironing board or iron.

Turn your fabric wrong side up and place your inter-lining over the material square, paper upwards, sticky side to the material, making sure there is no overhang to stick to the ironing board. Press with a dry iron.

Place your pattern pieces, mirror-reverse onto the paper backing, and trace around your patterns. Now cut these out.

Using a hard surface and your HB pencil or dressmaker's carbon, trace the extended lines of the wings on the hot pink fabric and the purple sections.

Lay the sections of the wings onto your background fabric and ascertain the position you want. Remove the protective paper backing from the hot pink section and place back into position. Remove the backing from the purple section and place on top of the hot pink section. Remove the backing from the green striped section and place it over the purple section.

Now, remove the paper backing from the green body and place over the pink wing section. Remove the backing from the dark green branch and slide it under the body. Now, remove the backing from the leaves and place those into position. Lastly, remove the backing of the yellow circles and place them into position.

Check that the position is correct and place unwaxed greaseproof paper over the design. Using a steam iron place the iron flat down onto one section of the design. Lift and repeat in same manner until all the design is firmly adhered to the background fabric. Do not slide the iron over your design until it is firmly adhered.

Place your design onto a hard surface and with your HB pencil draw in the antennae.

Place unwaxed greaseproof paper behind your background fabric and prepare your machine for stitching.

Stitching Procedure

Thread your machine with hot pink cotton, and wind your bobbin with the same colour, unless you intend white for all colours. (If you set your tension at 3, the white will not show through.)

Secure thread and starting at the top right-hand side (RHS) of the bottom wing stitch down to the body. Secure thread and go to the second line of the bottom wing. Secure thread and come down to the body making sure you follow the curved line. Secure thread.

Turn your design upside down and start at the body. Secure thread and stitch the third line of the bottom wing. Leaving your design upside down, complete the last line of the wing.

Change cotton for the purple section and start at the right-hand side (RHS). Come down the edge of the purple section, pivot and come across the top of the hot pink section. Secure thread and go to the top of the second line. Secure thread and come down that line. Pivot at corner and come across the top of the middle of the hot pink section. Pivot at corner and come back up the middle section. Secure thread and come back down to the last purple section. Secure thread and come across the hot pink section. Pivot at corner and come back up to outside edge of the purple section.

Change to lime green cotton and, starting at the right-hand side (RHS) of the striped section nearest the middle section, stitch to the corner. Pivot and come down the outside of this section. Pivot and come across the top of the purple section.

For the middle section, start at the narrowest point. Reduce your stitch width slightly and come across the top of the purple section, pivot at corner and come back across the top of the striped section, reducing as you reach the narrow point. Secure thread. For the last striped section, secure thread and come across the purple section. Pivot at corner and come up the outside edge. Pivot and come back to join up with the middle section.

Reduce your stitch width for the body and start at the left-hand side (LHS) top edge coming around the curve of the head. Pivot and go back around to come back to the narrow end. Reduce stitch width as you come. Secure thread.

For the lime green leaves, you will need to reduce your stitch width at the start and finish. Secure thread at each end.

Now, change to dark green cotton and secure thread for the branch. Start at the top line nearest the head of body, coming round and out for the branches and reducing stitch width for each one. Work your way around the branch until you come back to the body on the LHS. Pivot at corners.

Change to sea green cotton and finish the sea green leaves in the same manner as the lime green leaves. Change to yellow and secure the thread. Do each circle on the wings.

Change to black and secure thread. Stitch the antennae, extending the stitch width up to approximately 4 for the last few stitches to represent the eyes.

If you wish to use this design for a garment, you could stitch sequins onto the circles for a touch of glamour.

TASHA THE CAT

Tasha The Cat Master Design

Materials Required

Fabric

Quilt square	30 x 36 cm	(12 x 14 in)
Body (mauve)	25 x 36 cm	(10 x 14 in)
Bow (purple)	6 x 16 cm	(2 x 6 in)
Bow centre	4 x 4 cm	(2 x 2 in)
Eyes	4 x 8 cm	(2 x 3 in)
Eyelids	3 x 6 cm	(1 x 3 in)
Tongue	3 x 3 cm	(1 x 1 in)
Pupils	4 x 4 cm	(2 x 2 in)
Nose	2 x 2 cm	(1 x 1 in)

Double-sided iron-on interlining
Dressmaker's carbon, tracing wheel
Unwaxed greaseproof paper
HB pencil
Cotton thread to match or highlight

Head and Tie Detail

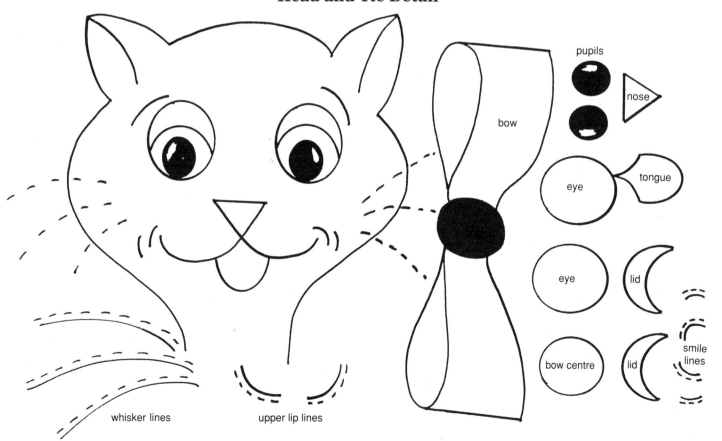

whisker lines   upper lip lines

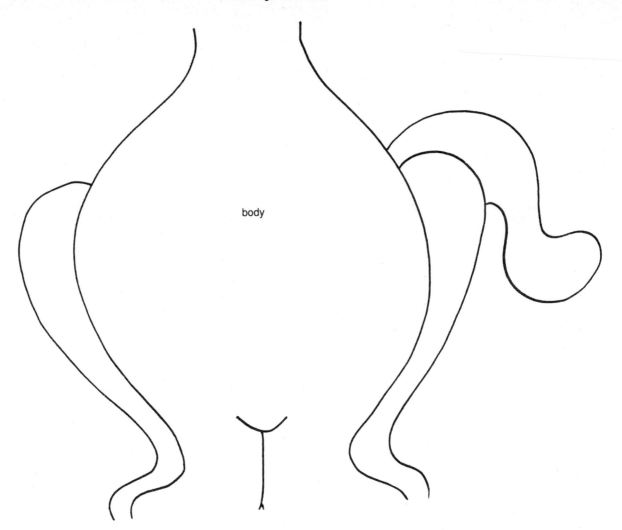

body

Construction Procedure

Measure out required amounts of fabric. Mark out your pattern pieces and cut approximate squares of each colour.

Cut out similar squares of your double-sided iron-on interlining slightly smaller than your material squares so it will not stick to your ironing board or iron.

Turn your fabric wrong side up and place your interlining over the material square, paper upwards, sticky side to the material, making sure there is no overhang to stick to the ironing board. Press with a dry iron.

Place your pattern pieces mirror-reverse onto the paper backing, and trace around your patterns. Now cut these out.

Using a hard surface and your HB pencil or dressmaker's carbon, trace the inside lines and facial lines. Place the eyes into position together with the nose to ascertain their correct position.

Now, lay the head into approximate position on your background material and then place the body into position. When you have decided on the correct position, peel off the protective paper backing, and press down with your hand for a minute. The heat of your hand will hold it in place. Now, peel off backing of the bow and place it into position and then the centre of bow and tongue. The tongue should sit just on the pencil line of the mouth with the nose directly above it.

If you find it necessary to make some adjustments to the curve of the tongue, do so before you remove the paper backing.

Place the white of the eyes with the pupil just on the edge of the white and the same with the purple lid. Again you may need to do some trimming of the lid for a perfect fit and do so before you remove the paper backing. Your design should now be ready for pressing with your steam iron.

Place a piece of unwaxed greaseproof paper over your design, and holding your iron firmly down onto one section of the design, hold a few seconds until the design is firmly adhered to the background fabric. Repeat the same procedure until the entire cat and bow has been affixed to the background.

Place unwaxed greaseproof paper behind your background fabric and prepare your machine for stitching.

Stitching Procedure

Thread your machine with mauve cotton and wind your bobbin with the same colour, unless you intend to use a white bobbin for all colours. (If you set your tension at 3, the white will not show through.)

Start at the left-hand side (LHS) above the bow. Come around the curve of the cheek, pivot and do the ear. Pivot at tip and at the corner near head. Secure thread and repeat same for the right-hand side (RHS).

Starting at the RHS under the bow, stitch the inner line of the body which includes the front paws. Approach the curved section slowly. If you have a slow button use this now, and pivot regularly around the paw. Stop at the straight section and secure thread. Now, move to the top of the straight section and come down the straight line and around the left paw and inner body line and back to the bow.

Secure thread and start on the right hind leg and then the tail. Secure thread. Now complete the left hind leg.

Outlining the bow start at the RHS at the top of the straight line. Start your stitching just inside the outline for the curved top section as this will allow you to just cover that stitching when you do the curved section. Pivot when you reach the corner and come back to the centre of the bow. Repeat the same for the LHS, securing thread at the curved section.

Starting at the centre of the bow, reduce your stitch width and then increase it to approximately 3 1/2 as you reach the centre of the bow's curve, and again reduce it as you come back around and secure thread. Repeat the same with the RHS curved section. Secure thread.

Now do the facial expressions. Secure thread before and after and use your slow button, if you have one, and carefully follow your pencil lines. It is necessary to go very carefully when doing facial lines as the curve is usually a tight one and it is easy to spoil the effect if your line does not follow the curve exactly. If you should find your line is going straight, stop and unpick. It is worth the effort to do it again.

Change to hot pink cotton for the centre of the bow. Secure thread and pivot regularly around the circle.

When doing the tongue, place your needle just on the mouth line, secure thread and slowly come around the curve. Pivot where necessary and go back to the mouth line, stopping just on the line once again and secure thread. Do not stitch over the mouth line as it will cause bumps when you stitch over it in black.

Now start on the upper lid with the stitch width at 3. Do not reduce here as the white stitching must be the same as the black and mauve stitching. Go around the eye carefully, pivot regularly and secure thread. Change to black and do the pupils. Again pivot regularly and secure thread.

Now go to the nose, secure thread and start at the LHS of the nose. Come across the straight section first and back down the LHS curve to form the mouth.

Secure thread and repeat the same for the RHS, making sure that you completely cover the pink tongue by going very slowly. If you find it is not covering, you can either close up the stitch a little or go over it twice. If you choose to close up the stitch length, remember to adjust back to normal when you finish.

If your background fabric is stretch, place either a folded piece of backing paper or some thicker interlining which you can pull off later when you do the whiskers. This will give you a thicker whisker and an even straight edge. If it is stretch you are using, it is preferable to go over the line twice rather than closing up the stitch.

Change to purple and do the upper lids. Do not reduce at ends. Secure at start and finish. You may find it necessary to pivot occasionally.

MRS MOUSE

Face and Inner Ear Detail

eye

pupil

whisker lines

nose   tooth   mouth

face

left eye lines

hair lines

Mrs Mouse Master Design

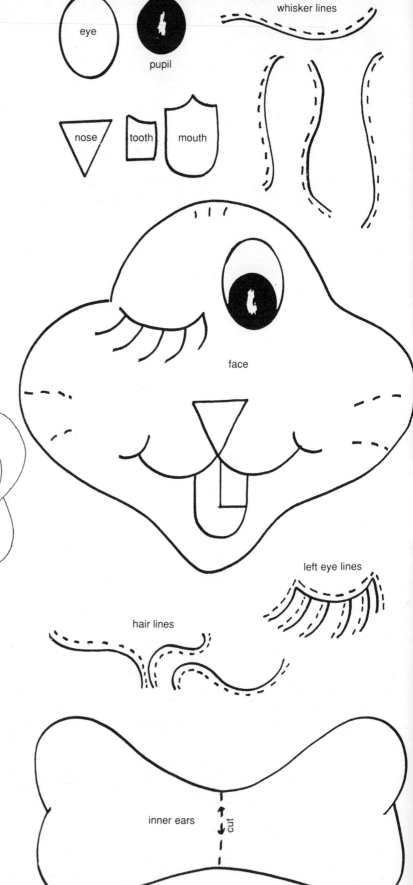

inner ears   cut

Body and Outer Ear Detail

outer ears

cut

body

tail

Materials Required

Fabric

Quilt square	30 x 36 cm	(12 x 14 in)
Hot pink	8 x 14 cm	(3 x 6 in)
Grey cotton	26 x 35 cm	(10 x 14 in)
Grey corduroy	14 x 35 cm	(6 x 14 in)
Scraps of white and black		

Double-sided iron-on interlining
Dressmaker's carbon, tracing wheel
Unwaxed greaseproof paper
HB pencil
Cotton thread to match or highlight

Construction Procedure

Measure out required amounts of fabric. Mark out your pattern pieces and cut approximate squares of each colour.

Cut out similar squares of your double-sided iron-on interlining slightly smaller so it will not stick to your ironing board or iron.

Turn your fabric wrong side up and place your interlining over the material square, paper upwards, sticky side to the material, making sure there is no overhang to stick to the ironing board. Press with a dry iron.

Place your pattern pieces, mirror-reverse onto the paper backing, and trace round your patterns. Now cut these out.

Using a hard surface and your HB pencil or dressmaker's carbon, trace a light line where the eye will go. Then draw in the eyelashes a bit darker. Now draw in the mouth lines. After placing the nose into position, draw in the other facial lines. You will draw in the whiskers and hair after you have ironed the design.

Now, place the body into position and when you ascertain the correct position, peel off the protective paper backing and replace. Now, remove the paper backing from the ears and place them under the face. Now, place the tail under the body and remove the backing from the arm and place it into position. Now, peel off the backing from the inner ears and place them over the outer ears and under the face.

Place a piece of unwaxed greaseproof paper over the mouse design and using a steam iron, hold it down over the head and ears. Lift and place down over each section of the design until it is completely adhered to the background fabric.

Now, proceed to place the eye into position and then the nose. If you need to trim the tongue and tooth to fit into the curve of the mouth, do so before you take off the paper backing. Once you have these in the correct position, place a piece of unwaxed greaseproof paper over the face and press with a steam iron as before.

Now draw in the whiskers and hair lines.

Place unwaxed greaseproof paper behind your background fabric and prepare your machine for stitching.

Stitching Procedure

Thread your machine with grey cotton and wind your bobbin with the same colour, unless you intend to use white for all colours. (If you set your tension at 3, the white will not show through.) Set your stitch width at 3 to 3 1/2 and your length at 1/2.

Start at the right-hand side (RHS) of the cheek and go around the head. Then start at the RHS of the neck and stitch round the feet until you finish at the left-hand side (LHS) of the neck. Pivot around the feet.

Now, start on the ears and don't forget to extend the curved line. Secure thread. Complete both ears in the same manner. Now, go to the tail. Secure thread and reduce the stitch as you come to the end of the tail. Secure thread and go to the arm. Pivot around the rounded end of the arm and the fist. Secure thread.

Now, change to hot pink cotton for the inner ears. Secure thread and proceed in the same manner as the outer ears.

For the tongue, insert your needle just on the line of the tongue and secure thread and pivot as you come around the tongue. Secure thread when you reach the mouth line. Do not stitch the top of the tongue as it will be covered in black.

Change to white for the eye and tooth. For the tooth, insert your needle just below the mouth line and secure thread. Come down to the corner, pivot and go across the base of the tooth. Pivot and come back up the other side to the mouth line and secure thread.

For the eye, I turned the design upside down and started on the LHS (which is now the RHS) of the white. I reduced the stitch width to start and secured the thread, came around the eye pivoting regularly to form an even stitch, and back to the black pupil again reducing the stitch width so it will fit perfectly into the black.

Now change to black and do the nose first. Secure thread and start at the LHS of the nose, come across the top and down the RHS and into the curve of the mouth stitching right to the end of your pencil lines. Repeat the same for the other side. Now, go to the pupil, pivot regularly and cover the start of the white stitching. Secure thread.

For the eyelashes, you need a good strong pencil line to be able to see it as you sew. Secure thread and do the top line from the LHS to the RHS. Pivot at corner and come down for the first lash. Take care to get the full curve and follow the line carefully. Secure thread and go to the second curve and repeat the same for all lashes. Secure at each end. If you have not been able to get the curve, unpick and try again.

It is not easy to get a good curve, therefore you must take it slowly and place each needle on the pencil line. You should use your slow button if you have one.

Now, go to the whiskers. When you do the whiskers on the face you will get good coverage, but when you go off the face and onto the background fabric, particularly if it is stretch, you will need to go over that section twice. You can place extra paper under that section before you stitch or use some thicker interlining and pull it off the back later. I prefer to use the interlining, as I get the best results with it.

The same applies for the hair lines that usually need to stitched twice.

This is one of my favourite designs and I love to wear it, because it always gets a grin out of someone. I also use the same size mouse for children from about 6 onwards.

UNICORN

Materials Required

Fabric

Quilt square	30 x 36 cm	(12 x 14 in)
White body	20 x 25 cm	(8 x 10 in)
Top of wing	10 x 17 cm	(4 x 7 in)
Pink mane	6 x 6 cm	(3 x 3 in)
Green mane	6 x 6 cm	(3 x 3 in)
Green tail	8 x 8 cm	(3 x 3 in)
Pink tail	8 x 8 cm	(3 x 3 in)
Royal blue	4 x 10 cm	(2 x 4 in)
Purple	4 x 14 cm	(2 x 6 in)
Mauve	4 x 14 cm	(2 x 6 in)
Hot pink	4 x 12 cm	(2 x 5 in)
Green	4 x 10 cm	(2 x 4 in)
Yellow	2 x 10 cm	(1 x 4 in)

Double-sided iron-on interlining
Dressmaker's carbon, tracing wheel
Unwaxed greaseproof paper
HB pencil
Cotton thread to match or highlight

Unicorn Master Design

Wing Detail

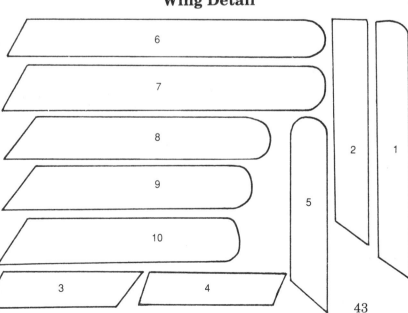

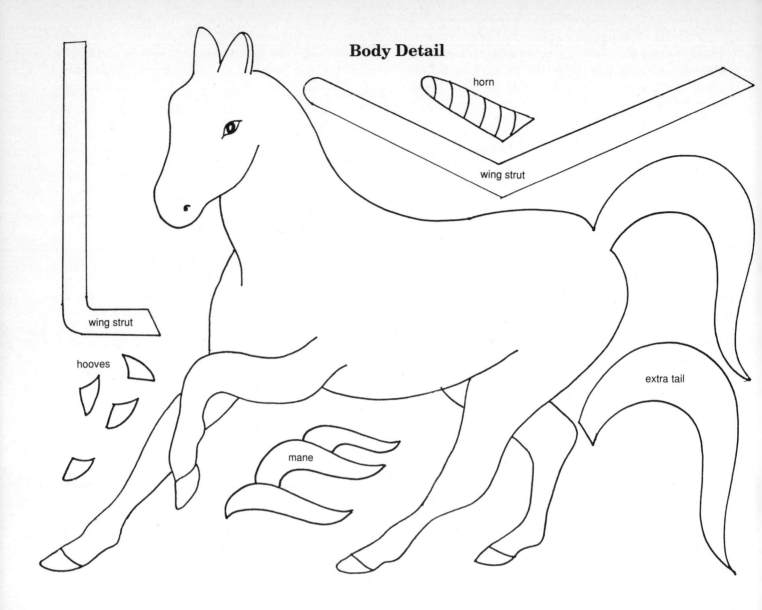

Body Detail

horn

wing strut

wing strut

hooves

mane

extra tail

Construction Procedure

Measure out required amounts of fabric. Mark out your pattern pieces and cut approximate squares of each colour.

Cut out similar squares of your double-sided iron-on interlining slightly smaller than your material squares so it will not stick to your ironing board or iron.

Turn your fabric wrong side up and place your inter-lining over the material square, paper upwards, sticky side to the material, making sure there is no overhang to stick to the ironing board. Press with a dry iron.

Place your pattern pieces, mirror-reverse onto the paper backing, and trace around your patterns. Now cut these out.

Using a hard surface and your HB pencil or dressmaker's carbon, trace out the leg lines of the horse and then head and neck lines.

Now, ascertain where the unicorn will sit on your material. Once you have the correct position, peel off the protective paper backing and hold down firmly with your hand. The heat of your hand will make it sit more firmly. Now, peel off the paper backing and place the pink tail and slide it under the rump. Remove the backing from the green tail and slide it under the rump and behind the pink tail.

Now, peel off the backing and place the white top wing into position. Then slide the rear wing under the head and under the top wing. Now, after carefully removing the backing, slide the blue section under the white top wing on both wings. Remove the backing and slide the purple section under the blue section on both wings. Remove the backing from mauve section and slide it under the purple section on both wings. Remove the backing on hot pink sections and slide them under the mauve sections. Remove the backing from the green sections and slide them under the hot pink sections. Remove the yellow backing and slide it under the green section.

These can be a bit fiddly. Try using a pair of tweezers to place the sections. Now, place the hot pink mane into position over the ends of the rear wing and then place the green mane over the hot pink mane so the start is just under the ear. Lastly, place the horn just over the left ear, but in the middle of forehead.

Check that all is in place. Put a piece of unwaxed greaseproof paper over the design and hold your steam iron down over one section of the design. Hold for a few seconds and remove. Repeat this procedure until the entire design is firmly affixed to the background material.

Now, one at a time remove the paper backing of the hooves. Using tweezers place these onto the legs. In this instance you can steam-press each one as you go.

Place unwaxed greaseproof paper behind your background fabric and prepare your machine for stitching.

Stitching Procedure

Thread your machine with white cotton and wind your bobbin with the same colour. (If you set your tension at 3, the white will not show through on the other colours.)

Starting at the right-hand side (RHS) of the body, secure thread and come around the rump and down the front rear leg, securing thread at hoof. Go to the other side of the hoof, secure thread and come back up to the belly. Secure thread and do the small section of the rear leg.

Insert your needle right on the belly line and stitch to the front rear leg, secure thread. Come over to the rear line of the rear leg, secure thread and stitch around the rear leg. Secure thread at hoof. Go to the other side of the hoof, secure thread and come back up the rear leg. Secure thread.

Now, come across to the front leg, secure thread and come down the back line of leg stopping at hoof and secure thread. Go across to the other side of hoof and come back up the front line of the leg and secure thread. Do the small section of the rear front leg and secure thread. You may need to reduce your stitch width to butt right up to the other stitching.

Come back to the belly. Now, secure thread and stitch around the belly. Secure thread when you reach the leg.

Do the front rear leg in the same manner as the other leg and secure thread. Now, turn your design upside down, secure thread and do the curved sections of neck.

Secure thread. Turn your design right side up and stitch the head taking care with the curves. Pivot at each curve to give a definite line stopping at the horn and secure thread.

Change to green and proceed with the horn. Secure thread and pivot at corners. Pivot regularly around the top of horn, and back down to start.

Go to the mane and secure thread. Come down the curve, reducing your stitch width at each end. Secure thread at the end of each section.

Now, go to the tail, secure thread and come down the tail. As you reach the hot pink section of the curve, reduce your stitch width right down so you have a small stitch outlining the tail. Increase the width back up, and back down for the tip. Pivot and come back up to the pink tail. Secure thread.

Now, go to the wing and do the green sections. Secure thread and come across the wing. Pivot around the curved section, and do only one side of each colour. Complete the rear wing in green.

Change to blue and do both wings in the same manner. Continue in this manner with each colour until you complete both wings. Remember to secure at start and finish off each colour.

When you reach the hot pink colour, do the mane in the same manner as the green. There may be some small sections so reduce your stitch width accordingly. Secure thread.

Now, change to black and reduce your stitch width to approximately 2 3/4. Secure your thread at the rear hoof. Come down to the corner, pivot and come across the bottom of hoof, pivot and back up to the front of hoof, pivot and come back to the beginning. Secure thread and repeat the same for each hoof.

For the eyes, you can either embroider by hand using a satin stitch or use the machine. If using the machine, reduce your stitch width right down and secure thread. You will need to increase the width quickly and evenly and then back down again and secure thread.

For the nostril, I secured thread and decreased the stitch width right down. Holding the design steady, I quickly increased the stitch width but at the same time stitched in a half-moon. I then reduced the stitch width right down again and secured the thread. It is not easy to do this and I think I fluked it. It would be easier to do it by hand using small satin stitches.

BOY'S QUILT

This quilt has been made from a series of individual designs. The final layout of the quilt is left up to you. The designs can be used individually on sweatshirts, childrens' clothes or any item you like.

The pattern details have been reduced to 75%. See page 10 for instructions on enlarging them to full size.

Materials Required

Fabric

Quilt square	25 x 37 cm	(10 x 15 in)
Calico	13 x 22 cm	(5 x 9 in)
Dark green	12 x 27 cm	(5 x 11 in)
Green spot	12 x 12 cm	(5 x 5 in)
Brown	4 x 12 cm	(2 x 5 in)
White	10 x 22 cm	(4 x 9 in)
Red	6 x 7 cm	(3 x 3 in)
Yellow	6 x 12 cm	(3 x 5 in)
Cinnamon	7 x 16 cm	(3 x 7 in)

Double-sided iron-on interlining
Dressmaker's carbon, tracing wheel
Unwaxed greaseproof paper
HB pencil
Cotton thread to match or highlight

Dinosaur Master Design

46

Body and Foreground Detail

cloud

shrub

tree top

trunk

grass

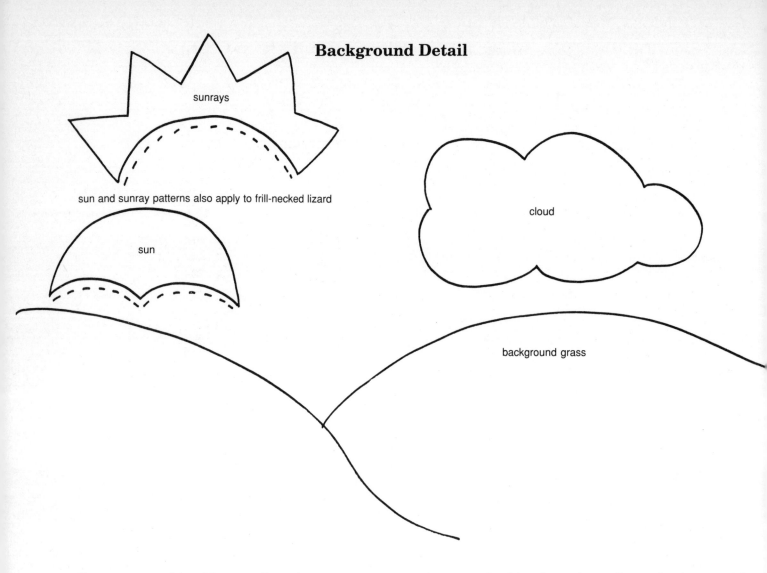

Background Detail

sunrays

sun and sunray patterns also apply to frill-necked lizard

sun

cloud

background grass

Construction Procedure

Measure out required amounts of fabric. Mark out your pattern pieces and cut approximate squares of each colour.

Cut out similar squares of your double sided iron-on interlining slightly smaller so it will not stick to your ironing board or iron.

Turn your fabric wrong side up and place your interlining over the material square, paper upwards, sticky side to the material, making sure there is no overhang to stick to the ironing board. Press with a dry iron.

Place your pattern pieces, mirror-reverse onto the paper backing, and trace around your patterns. Now cut these out.

Using a hard surface and your HB pencil or dressmaker's carbon, trace the extended lines of the dinosaur's back and the internal lines of the legs.

Lay out the background pieces first. Once you have established where you want them, remove the protec-tive paper backing from them. Cover the design with unwaxed greaseproof paper and press with a steam iron. Do not allow the iron to slide. Lift iron and hold down on each section until the complete design adheres to the background fabric. Remember to slide the bushes under the green hill before you press.

Now, peel off the backing from the dinosaur and place over the hills. Remove the backing from the cinnamon fins and place under the calico fins. When position is correct, press with a steam iron as before.

Place unwaxed greaseproof paper behind your background fabric and prepare your machine for stitching.

Stitching Procedure

Thread your machine with the colour for the outline of the dinosaur and wind the bobbin in the same colour, unless you intend to use a white bobbin for all colours. (If you set your tension at 3, the white will not show through.)

Starting at the first of the smallest fins, secure thread and pivot at the tip and at the base of the two fins. Come down the head, pivot at the nose and at the tip of the nose. Come down around the underneath of the dinosaur, pivot at each curve and stop at the legs.

Secure thread and start at the top of the legs. Pivot at curves and come across the bottom of the leg and back up the outside line. Do the internal lines later.

Now, do the belly and the back legs in the same manner as the front legs. Now, come around the tail and start on the larger fins in the same manner as the smaller ones. Now, do the internal lines.

Change to your contrast colour for contrast fins and complete those. Change to dark green and do the dark green hills. Now, complete the lime green hills. Change to a contrast colour for the bushes and tree top and complete. Pivot around each curve. Now, change to white for the clouds and pivot around their curves. Change to red and complete the sun. Now change to yellow and stitch the rays in the same manner as you stitched the fins.

Finally, change to black and put 6 to 8 small stitches in for the eye or you can hand-embroider them.

JET PLANE

Materials Required

Fabric

Quilt square	25 x 37 cm	(10 x 15 in)
White	10 x 20 cm	(4 x 8 in)
Blue spot	20 x 20 cm	(8 x 8 in)
Blue	6 x 22 cm	(3 x 9 in)
Red	8 x 8 cm	(3 x 3 in)

Double-sided iron-on interlining
Dressmaker's carbon, tracing wheel
Unwaxed greaseproof paper
HB pencil
Cotton thread to match or highlight

Jet Plane Master Design

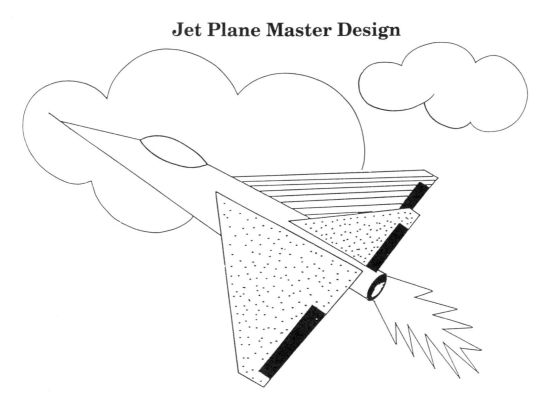

Jet Plane Detail

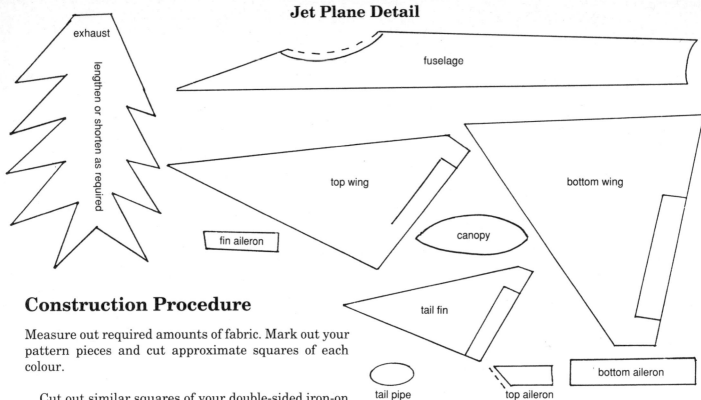

exhaust

lengthen or shorten as required

fuselage

top wing

bottom wing

fin aileron

canopy

tail fin

bottom aileron

tail pipe

top aileron

Construction Procedure

Measure out required amounts of fabric. Mark out your pattern pieces and cut approximate squares of each colour.

Cut out similar squares of your double-sided iron-on interlining slightly smaller so it will not stick to your ironing board or iron.

Turn your fabric wrong side up and place your interlining over the material square, paper upwards, sticky side to the material, making sure there is no overhang to stick to the ironing board. Press with a dry iron.

Place your pattern pieces, mirror-reverse onto the paper backing, and trace around your patterns. Now cut these out.

Place your clouds onto the design first. Now lay out your jet pieces carefully. Place the jet so it looks like it is flying up into the clouds. Once you ascertain the position you want, carefully remove the pieces of the jet and remove the paper backing from the clouds and then reassemble the jet pieces. Carefully remove paper backing from jet pieces as you place them.

Lay the fuselage first, then place the top wing under the fuselage and the bottom wing over the fuselage. Now place the tail fin over the fuselage and then place the canopy over the fuselage. Now place the three blue ailerons (hinged flaps). Now place the red exhaust.

When you have reassembled the design, place unwaxed greaseproof paper over it and press with a stream iron. Lift iron and hold down over all sections until the design adheres completely to the background.

Place unwaxed greaseproof paper behind your background fabric and prepare your machine for stitching.

Stitching Procedure

Thread your machine with light blue cotton and wind your bobbin with the same colour, unless you intend to use a white bobbin for all colours. (If you set your tension at 3, the white will not show through.

Set your stitch width at 3 and start at the bottom line of the top wing nearest the tail fin. Stitch to the corner and pivot and come back up the wing. Pivot at top and stop at blue aileron and secure thread. Come down and stitch the tail fin in same manner.

Now, starting at the bottom edge of the aileron on the bottom wing, stitch down to corner, pivot and come back up and around the wing. Secure thread and now complete the canopy.

Now change to royal blue cotton and do the short section between the exhaust flame and the wing. Secure thread and then go to the other side of the wing and pivot at tip of nose, back up to the canopy and secure. Now complete the three ailerons, pivot at each corner and secure at each end.

Change to white, complete the clouds and pivot around the curves. Change to red and carefully using your slow button, if you have one, pivot around the circle. Now start on the flame. Reduce at each peak and pivot at inside peak. Secure. Change to black and stitch the short black section on the nose.

MR HIPPO

Materials Required

Fabric

Quilt square size	25 x 37 cm	(10 x 15 in)
Grey	20 x 22 cm	(4 x 6 in)
Corduroy	10 x 15 cm	(4 x 6 in)
Hot pink	4 x 8 cm	(2 x 3 in)
Red	3 x 6 cm	(1 x 3 in)
Yellow	3 x 3 cm	(1 x 1 in)
Lime green	7 x 12 cm	(3 x 5 in)
Black	8 x 16 cm	(3 x 6 in)
White		

Double-sided iron-on interlining
Dressmaker's carbon, tracing wheel
Unwaxed greaseproof paper
HB pencil
Cotton thread to match or highlight
Black embroidery cotton
Green embroidery cotton

Mr Hippo Master Design

Head and Body Detail

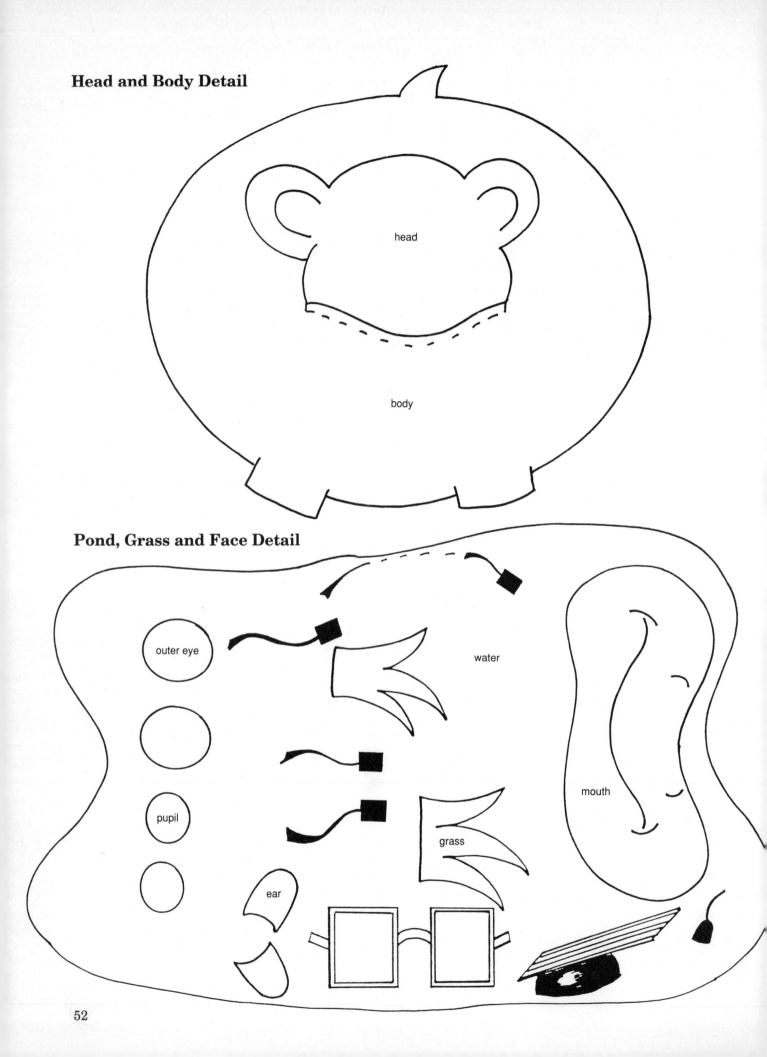

head

body

Pond, Grass and Face Detail

outer eye

water

pupil

mouth

grass

ear

Construction Procedure

Measure out required amounts of fabric. Mark out your pattern pieces and cut approximate squares of each colour.

Cut out similar squares of your double-sided iron-on interlining slightly smaller so it will not stick to your ironing board or iron.

Turn your fabric wrong side up, place your interlining over the material square, paper upwards, sticky side to the material, making sure there is no overhang to stick to the ironing board. Press with a dry iron.

Place your pattern pieces, mirror-reverse onto the paper backing, and trace around your patterns. Now cut these out.

Now, lay your garment on a hard surface and, using your HB pencil or dressmaker's carbon, trace in the face. Mark where the eyes will go and mark in the brows. Draw in the mouth lines on the corduroy. Mark in the water lines on the blue water.

Lay out the design onto the fabric and ascertain the position you want. Carefully remove the water and remove the paper backing and replace. Now, place the hippo over the water with the tail under the body. Place the mouth into position remembering to remove the paper backing from these parts.

Now, remove the backing from the inner ears and place into position. Place the reeds into position. Now, remove the backing from the white of the eye and place into position. Now place the black pupil over the white eye. Place hat in position but leave glasses.

Once you have everything in position place unwaxed greaseproof paper over the design and steam-press. Lift and press until the entire design adheres to the background.

Place unwaxed greaseproof paper behind your background fabric and prepare your machine for stitching.

Stitching Procedure

Thread your machine with the colour you have chosen for the hippo and wind your bobbin in the same colour unless you intend to use a white bobbin for all colours. (If you set your tension at 3, the white will not show through.)

Start with the legs. Secure thread and come down the legs, across the bottom of leg and secure thread. Now, start on the belly, secure thread, and come across to the left leg. Stitch that and come around the outside of the body across the tail and right around until you come to the leg again and secure thread.

Now, starting at the left-hand side (LHS) of the face, turn your design upside down and secure thread. Pivot around the cheek and the ears and back to the mouth on the other side. Now, complete the mouth. Finish the tail.

Change to blue and start on the right-hand side (RHS) of the water. Come around to the other side, pivot at each curve and secure thread. Now do the internal water lines and secure thread.

Change to lime green and stitch the stems of the flowers. Reduce at tip of reeds, doing the front ones first and then filling in the back ones.

Now, change to red and do the red sections of the flowers and then the yellow. Now change to hot pink, stitch the inner ears and pivot around curves. Now change to white and stitch the eyes. Do not go over the black pupil but reduce your stitch width into the black. Change to black and finish the pupil and mouth lines.

For the hat, insert your needle up against the top and stitch the curved section first. Pivot at corners and finish just under the top of the hat. Now complete the straight sections and pivot at corners. For the tassel, reduce your stitch width to 2 for the cord and increase the width to 4 for the tassel. Secure thread at finish.

For the glasses, I set my stitch width at 3 1/2 and stitched an outline of the glasses. Take care to stitch them straight, I found it easier to do them this way. You may do it either way, but do not make them too bulky or they will dominate the face and spoil the design.

Lastly, do the flower in the hippo's mouth. I set my stitch width at 3 1/2 to 4 and reduced it down to 0 at the black mouth line and secured thread. I then started on the other side of the black line, secured thread and reduced the stitch width down to 0 and quickly increased it to 2. Secure thread and do the tip of the flower in whatever colour you choose.

FRILL-NECKED LIZARD

Frill Neck Detail

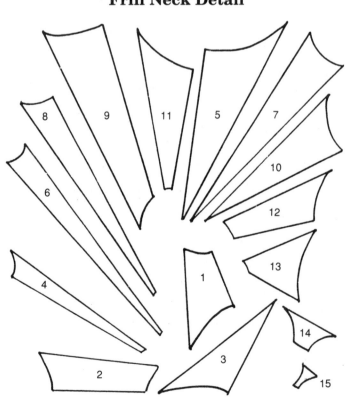

Materials Required

Fabric

Quilt square	25 x 37 cm	(10 x 15 in)
Brown	8 x 37 cm	(3 x 14 in)
Calico	22 x 30 cm	(9 x 12 in)
White	8 x 15 cm	(3 x 6 in)
Green	12 x 14 cm	(5 x 5 in)
Cinnamon	12 x 14 cm	(5 x 5 in)
Bark contrast	8 x 13 cm	(3 x 5 in)
Orange	4 x 10 cm	(2 x 4 in)
Cinnamon	10 x 15 cm	(4 x 6 in)
Bone belly	6 x 6 cm	(3 x 3 in)

Double sided iron-on interlining
Dressmaker's carbon, tracing wheel
Unwaxed greaseproof paper
HB pencil
Cotton thread to match or highlight
See Dinosaur design for details of the sun, cloud and
sun rays

Branch, Body and Grass Detail

branch

belly

body

bark

grass

Construction Procedure

Measure out required amounts of fabric. Mark out your pattern pieces and cut approximate squares of each colour.

Cut out similar squares of your double-sided iron-on interlining slightly smaller so it will not stick to your ironing board or iron.

Turn your fabric wrong side up and place your interlining over the material square, paper upwards, sticky side to the material, making sure there is no overhang to stick to the ironing board. Press with a dry iron.

Place your pattern pieces, mirror-reverse onto the paper backing, and trace around your pattern. Now cut these out.

Using a hard surface, and your HB pencil or dressmaker's carbon, trace in the lines of the frill.

Now, remove the paper backing from the tree trunk and place onto the background fabric. Remove the backing from the two different coloured grasses and place one behind the log and one in front.

Now, remove the paper backing from the frill-necked lizard and place on the log. Now place the belly into position. Remove the bark contrasts and place into position. Now place the cloud and sun in position.

Check that the design is all correct and then place unwaxed greaseproof paper over the design and steam-press. Now, carefully following the numbers, remove the paper backing one by one and place the contrast colour of the neck.

Press with a steam iron but do not allow the iron to slide. Lift iron and hold down until the centre design adheres to the background fabric.

Place unwaxed greaseproof paper behind your background fabric and prepare your machine for stitching.

Stitching Procedure

Thread your machine with a contrast colour for the frill and wind your bobbin in the same colour, unless you intend to use a white bobbin for all colours. (If you set your tension at 3, the white will not show through.)

Start on the top line of the mouth, secure thread and come around the nose and back around the head to join up with the first line. Pivot at each curve and corner.

Now, start under the mouth on the right-hand side (RHS) of the frill and pivot around each curve, stopping at each one to give a definite curve. Work your way to the other side and secure thread. Now, come back to the front leg and come down the leg reducing stitch width at ends of claws and secure at belly.

Leave belly and start at the back leg. Come around the back leg and secure thread. Start behind that leg and come down the tail. Reduce for tail tip and back up the back of the body. Now, do all the internal lines of the frill and secure at each end.

Change to brown for the log and secure at side of the frill. Now change to lime green for grass. Do the front pieces first, filling in the back ones after that. Reduce at tips and repeat the same for the brown grass.

Change to bark contrast colour, do each piece of bark and secure at each one. Now change to white for the cloud, secure and pivot around the curves.

Change to red and complete the sun. Change to yellow and stitch the rays of the sun. Pivot at each tip and secure. Hand-embroider the teeth and eye.

RUPERT THE FROG

Materials Required

Fabric

Quilt square	25 x 37 cm	(10 x 15 in)
Lime green	16 x 16 cm	(7 x 7 in)
Dark green	14 x 24 cm	(6 x 10 in)
Blue	20 x 27 cm	(8 x 11 in)
Yellow	10 x 16 cm	(4 x 6 in)
Red	3 x 10 cm	(1 x 4 in)
Green spot	8 x 20 cm	(3 x 8 in)
Hot pink	3 x 6 cm	(1 x 3 in)

Double-sided iron-on interlining
Dressmaker's carbon, tracing wheel
Unwaxed greaseproof paper
HB pencil
Cotton thread to match or highlight

Frog Detail

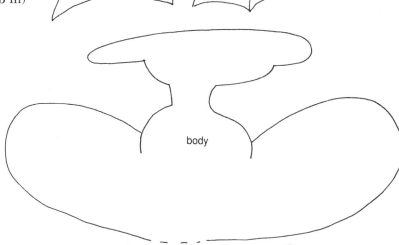

Rupert The Frog Master Design

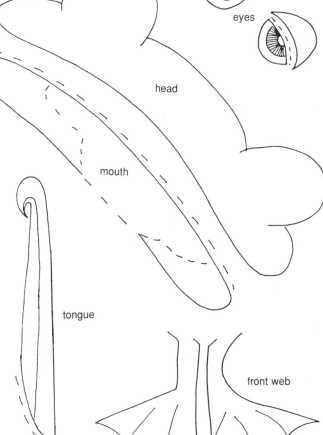

57

Pond and Lilypad Detail

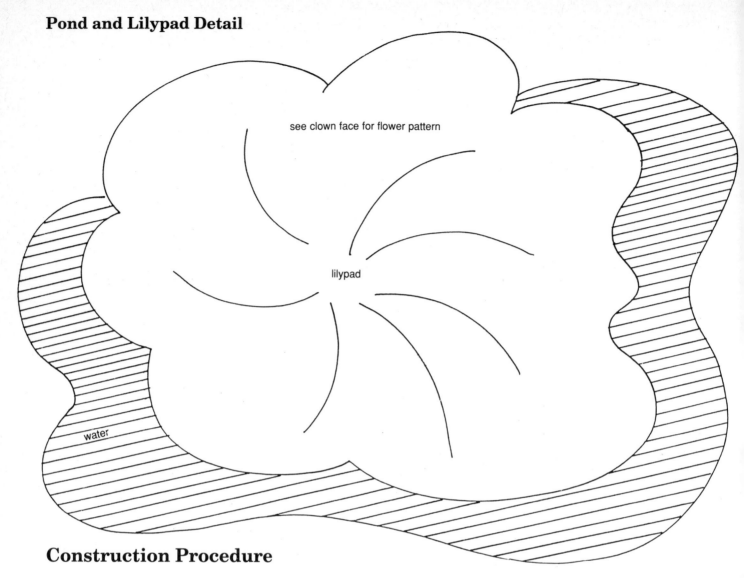

see clown face for flower pattern

lilypad

water

Construction Procedure

Measure out required amounts of fabric. Mark out your pattern pieces and cut approximate squares of each colour.

Cut out similar squares of your double-sided iron-on interlining slightly smaller so it will not stick to your ironing board or iron.

Turn your fabric wrong side up and place your interlining over the material square, paper upwards, sticky side to the material, making sure there is no overhang to stick to the ironing board. Press with a dry iron.

Place your pattern pieces, mirror-reverse onto the paper backing, and trace around your patterns. Now cut these out.

Using a hard surface and your HB pencil or dressmaker's carbon, trace the extended lines on the web feet, and the extended line in front of the back feet.

Lay out your design and remove the paper backing from the water and place into position. Now remove the

paper backing from the lily pad and place that over the water. Now remove the backing from the frog and place it into position. Slide the spotted section under the mouth and the spotted feet under the body and behind the front webbed feet.

Now, remove the backing from the tongue and place it under the mouth line. Now, place the green upper lid over the white eye and blue pupil. Lastly, place the flower and centre into position. Check that nothing has moved. Place unwaxed greaseproof paper over the design and press with a steam iron. Lift and press down until the entire design adheres to the background fabric.

Place unwaxed greaseproof paper behind your background fabric and prepare your machine for stitching.

Stitching Procedure

Thread your machine with lime green cotton and wind your bobbin in the same colour unless you use a white bobbin for all colours. (If you set your tension at 3, the white will not show through.)

58

Secure thread and start at the right eye. Come around the curve of the eye, pivot where necessary and come down and around the cheek and across the mouth and back up the other side. Pivot at curves and corners, complete and secure.

Now secure and do the short section between the mouth and the tongue. Secure thread and start on the other side of the tongue and come down around the body. Secure at end of extended line and start at the curve of the hind leg. Stop at the front foot and secure.

Come down the web and reduce at tip of web. Pivot at each curve and come back up the inside line of the web. Do the short section between the two webbed feet. Continue up the other side in the same manner as the right-hand side (RHS). Now, reduce stitch width and do the internal lines of the feet.

Change to dark green and do the lily pad and the upper lid of eye. Pivot around the eye and secure at end. Change to blue and do the water and the pupil. Pivot regularly around this small circle, as shown in chapter on circles. (See page 8)

Change to sea green and complete the mouth section and the web feet as before. Secure thread. Change to yellow and do the flower and then the centre. Change to red and stitch the tongue. Do the centre line first extend it right round the tongue, then blend the tip line into that.

Materials Required

Fabric

Quilt square size	25 x 37 cm	(10 x 15 in)
Royal blue	16 x 26 cm	(6 x 10 in)
White	17 x 26 cm	(7 x 10 in)
Black	2 x 10 cm	(1 x 4 in)
Red	8 x 8 cm	(3 x 3 in)

Double-sided iron-on interlining
Dressmaker's carbon, tracing wheel
Unwaxed greaseproof paper
HB pencil
Cotton thread to match or highlight

Aeroplane Master Design

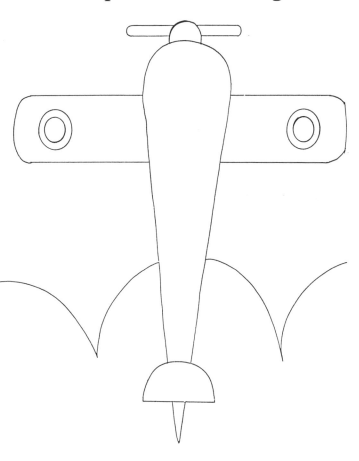

AEROPLANE

Tail and Marking Detail

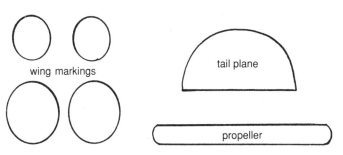

wing markings

tail plane

propeller

Cloud, Fuselage and Wing Detail

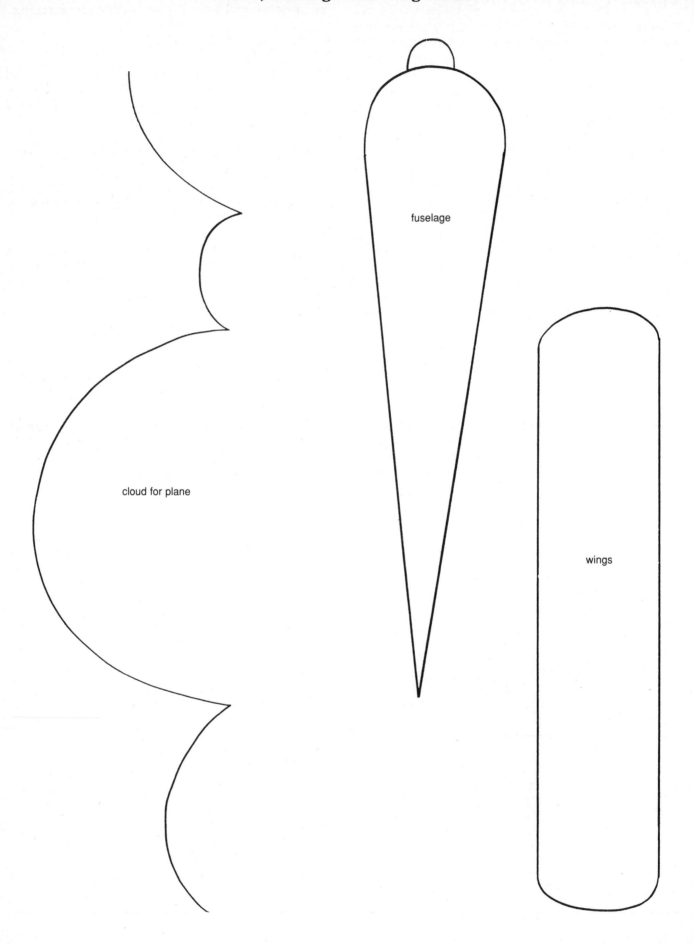

fuselage

wings

cloud for plane

Construction Procedure

Measure out required amounts of fabric. Mark out your pattern pieces and cut approximate squares of each colour.

Cut out similar squares of your double-sided iron-on interlining slightly smaller so it will not stick to your ironing board or iron.

Turning your fabric wrong side up, place your interlining over the material square, paper upwards, sticky side to the material, making sure there is no overhang to stick to the ironing board. Press with a dry iron.

Place your pattern pieces, mirror-reverse onto the paper backing, and trace around your patterns. Now cut these out.

Lay out your fabric and place the plane onto it and ascertain the correct position. Now, remove the paper backing from the cloud and place into position. Now, remove the backing from the fuselage and place it so the end of the tail is sitting halfway up the middle cloud.

Now, remove the backing from the wing and place it under the fuselage about 1 cm (1/2 in) below the nose cone. Remove the backing and place the tail plane about 1 cm (1/2 in) up from the tail tip. Slide the propeller under the nose cone. Lastly, remove the backing from the red and white circles and place them about 1 cm (1/2 in) from the wing tips, white on red.

When you have reassembled the design, place unwaxed greaseproof paper over it and press with a steam iron. Lift iron and hold down over all sections until the design adheres firmly to the background fabric.

Place unwaxed greaseproof paper behind your background fabric and prepare your machine for stitching.

Stitching Procedure

Thread your machine with royal blue thread, and wind the bobbin in the same colour, unless you intend to use a white bobbin for all colours. (If you set your tension at 3, the white will not show through.)

Starting about halfway down the fuselage on the right-hand side (RHS) secure your thread and set your stitch width at 3 and stitch down to the tail plane. Stop and secure thread and start on the other side of it. Secure and then start to reduce for the tail tip.

Pivot and slowly increase back up again, stopping at tail plane again. Secure at each side and continue up the left-hand side (LHS) of the plane. Pivot around the nose cone and back around to the starting point.

Now start on the right wing, secure thread and pivot around the wing tip and back again. Secure and repeat the same for the LHS. For the tail plane start at the RHS on the straight section, secure, and pivot at corners. Pivot around curve and secure.

Change to black and complete the propeller. Secure at each side of the nose cone and pivot at corners.

Change to red and complete the red circles. Pivot regularly and use your slow button if you have one.

Change to white and complete the clouds. Pivot around each curve and secure. Complete the design by doing the white circle. Pivot regularly and use your slow button, if you have one, and secure.

INTERNATIONAL STARS
OF SPORT
WALL-HANGING

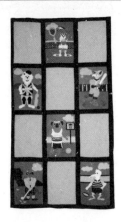

This wall-hanging has been made from a series of individual designs. The final layout of the wall-hanging is left up to you. The designs can be used individually on sweatshirts, childrens' clothes or any item you like.

The pattern details have been reduced to 75%. See page 10 for instructions on enlarging them to full size.

AUSTRALIAN KANGAROO TENNIS PLAYER

Australian Kangaroo Tennis Player Master Design

Arm and Pouch Detail

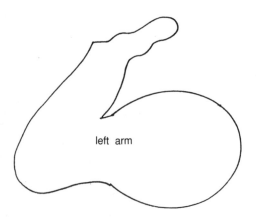

left arm

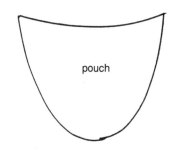

pouch

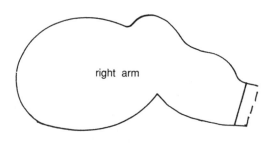

right arm

Body, Clothing and Equipment Detail

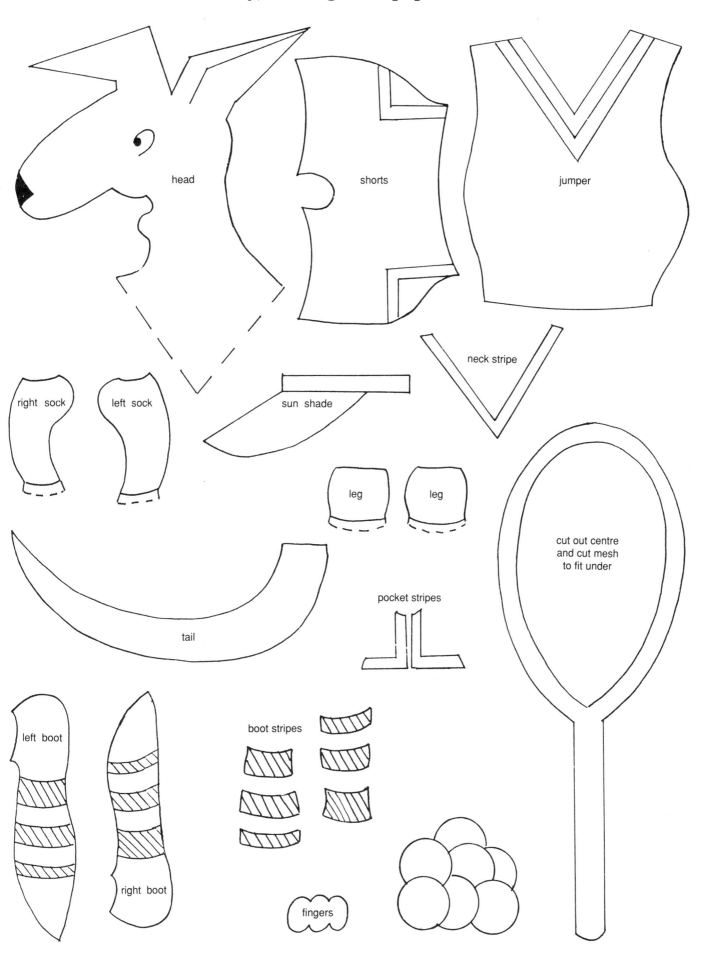

head

shorts

jumper

neck stripe

right sock

left sock

sun shade

leg

leg

cut out centre
and cut mesh
to fit under

tail

pocket stripes

left boot

boot stripes

right boot

fingers

Materials Required

Fabric

Quilt square	30 x 43 cm	(12 x 17 in)
Grey	12 x 32 cm	(5 x 13 in)
Red	14 x 20 cm	(6 x 8 in)
Gold	12 x 26 cm	(5 x 10 in)
White	6 x 7 cm	(3 x 3 in)
Green	10 x 10 cm	(4 x 4 in)
Lime green grass	22 x 31 cm	(9 x 12 in)
Sky	22 x 31 cm	(9 x 12 in)
Lime and white check net	7 x 31 cm	(3 x 12 in)
Black mesh to cover	7 x 31 cm	(3 x 12 in)
White cloud	10 x 14 cm	(4 x 6 in)

Double-sided iron-on interlining
Dressmaker's carbon, tracing wheel
Unwaxed greaseproof paper
HB pencil
Cotton thread to match or highlight
Black embroidery cotton
Refer to English lion for details of the net and cloud.

Construction Procedure

Measure out required amounts of fabric. Mark out your pattern pieces and cut approximate squares of each colour.

Cut out similar squares of your double-sided iron-on interlining slightly smaller so it will not stick to your ironing board or iron.

Turn your fabric wrong side up and place your interlining over the material squares, paper upwards, sticky side to the material, making sure there is no overhang to stick to the ironing board. Press with a dry iron.

Place your pattern pieces mirror-reverse onto the paper backing, and trace round your patterns. Now cut these out.

Using a hard surface and your HB pencil or dressmaker's carbon, trace the lines of eye and the outlines for the tennis balls.

For those making the quilt: Choose a light weight background fabric 31 x 44 cm (12 x 17 in) after pressing your interlining to background grass and sky, etc. Remove backing and press to background fabric.

Place the head, shirt, shorts, legs, etc. in position for the design. Once ascertained, remove the paper backing from the head and replace. Then remove the backing from the shirt and place over the neck of the kangaroo. Now, remove the backing from the shorts and place them over the shirt. Remove the backing from the tail and place it in the middle and under the shorts.

Now, place the arms over the edges of the shirt. Now, remove the backing from the legs and slide them under the shorts with the socks and shoes over each other.

Now, place the pouch halfway between shirt and shorts. Remove backing from the tennis balls and slide it under the top of the pouch. Now, place the mesh so it fits under the racket and slide it into position. Place the fingers around the racket handle after you have removed the paper backing.

Using tweezers, place the stripes on the shorts after removing backing. (I use tweezers for the fiddly pieces as the material sticks to your fingers and moves just as soon as you have placed it.)

Lastly, place the sun visor. Then place unwaxed greaseproof paper over your design and press with a steam iron. Lift and press until the entire design adheres to the fabric background.

Place unwaxed greaseproof paper behind your background fabric and prepare your machine for stitching.

Stitching Procedure

Thread your machine with grey, and wind your bobbin with the same colour, unless you intend to use a white bobbin for all colours. (If you set your tension at 3, the white will not show through.)

Set your stitch width at 3 and start at the inside of the right arm. Secure thread and stitch up arm and around the top. Pivot and come back to pouch. Secure thread. Now, start just below the left thumb. Secure and come around the bottom hand, pivot and carefully do the thumb. Secure thread and turn design upside down.

Start on the left-hand side (LHS) (now right-hand side RHS) of the neck nearest the jumper. Pivot carefully around the Adam's apple and stitch around to the visor. Secure thread and stitch the left ear and then right ear. Secure thread in between and do the inside line of the right ear. Secure thread.

Now go to the tail and secure thread and stitch down round the right outside edge of tail. Secure thread when you reach the leg, (both sides) and reduce your stitch width as you reach the tail tip. Pivot and come back up the other side in the same manner.

Now, go to the fingers. Secure thread and using your slow button, if you have one, carefully stitch around the fingers. Pivot at each curve and secure at end. (I decreased my stitch width to about 2 1/2 for the fingers.)

Change to gold thread. Secure and stitch the small sections at shoulder but do not cover the green stripe.

Boy's Quilt (see page 46).

Left: Mr Hippo from Boy's Quilt (see page 51); *right*: variation on Koala Basketball Player from International Stars of Sport Wall-hanging (see page 74); *front*: Jet Plane from Boy's Quilt (see page 49).

Come down the V, pivot and secure at shoulder. Start under the arm RHS, secure and come down the shirt. Do not cover the green stripe. Reduce thread for shorts and secure thread. Insert needle right up against the stripe and increase.

This time, cover the green stripe and come down around the shorts. Pivot regularly around the curve and back up to the green stripe. Cover bottom stripe and blend in to the green at the waist. Do not cover the waist stripe. Finish short.

For the boots, secure thread and start at the RHS of boot, pivot around the curve and cover ends of stripes. Reduce at the ends of the boots and back to the start. Repeat same for LHS of boot.

Starting at the RHS bottom line of the visor, secure thread and continue around visor. Reduce at peak and pivot. Secure at end.

Change to white thread, secure thread and start at the outside edge of the right sock. Pivot around the knee and secure at boot edge. Secure thread and come back up the inside of the right sock. Repeat same for left sock. Stitch the white section of the net and then the cloud. Pivot regularly around the cloud and secure.

Change to green thread. Secure thread at neck edge and outline the V. Come down and outline the pockets. Secure thread and reduce your stitch width to 2 3/4 and secure thread at edge of yellow.

For the stripes on the boots, I started with a stitch width of 3 1/4 for the widest stripe and reduced it down for each stripe. (As the stripe gets narrower so does the width of the stitch.)

Change to red thread and outline the racket. Secure thread at each side of hand. When stitching the inside of the racket, check that all parts of the mesh are enclosed under the red racket and secure thread.

For the tennis balls, make sure your pencil outlines are dark enough for you to see as you stitch. It is important that you take this section slowly and watch where your needle goes in. Use your slow button, if you have one, and start with the two outside balls at the bottom and work your way up.

If you are having difficulty in getting a rounded edge to your balls, you should unpick and try again. If you have not succeeded the second time, unpick it once again. Then leave it, go away and come back to it the next day.

This seems to work for me each time, some days you just do not seem to be as finely coordinated and yet on other days you can't put a stitch wrong. So don't throw it in the 'Too Hard Basket'. Give yourself some time and try again. You will get it with a little patience.

Change to black thread and encase the bottom edge of the black net. Now, for the nose I increased the stitch width to approximately 4 1/2. Secure thread and start at the largest part of nose, decrease the width down to about 1 1/2 at the tip of the nose and secure thread. For the eye, I set the stitch width at 3. Secure thread and stitch approximately 6 to 8 stitches. Quickly reduce width down to 2 and pivot around the eye outline. Secure at end.

For those who wish to hand-embroider the nose and eye, use a satin stitch for the nose and large part of the eye and use a stem stitch for the curve outline.

ENGLISH LION CRICKET PLAYER

English Lion Cricket Player Master Design

Hair and Face Detail

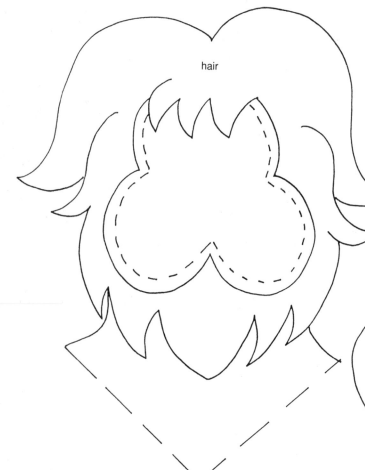

hair

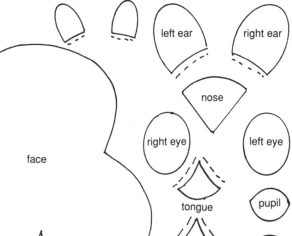

left inner ear   right inner ear

left ear   right ear

nose

right eye   left eye

face

tongue   pupil

mouth

66

Body and Clothing Detail

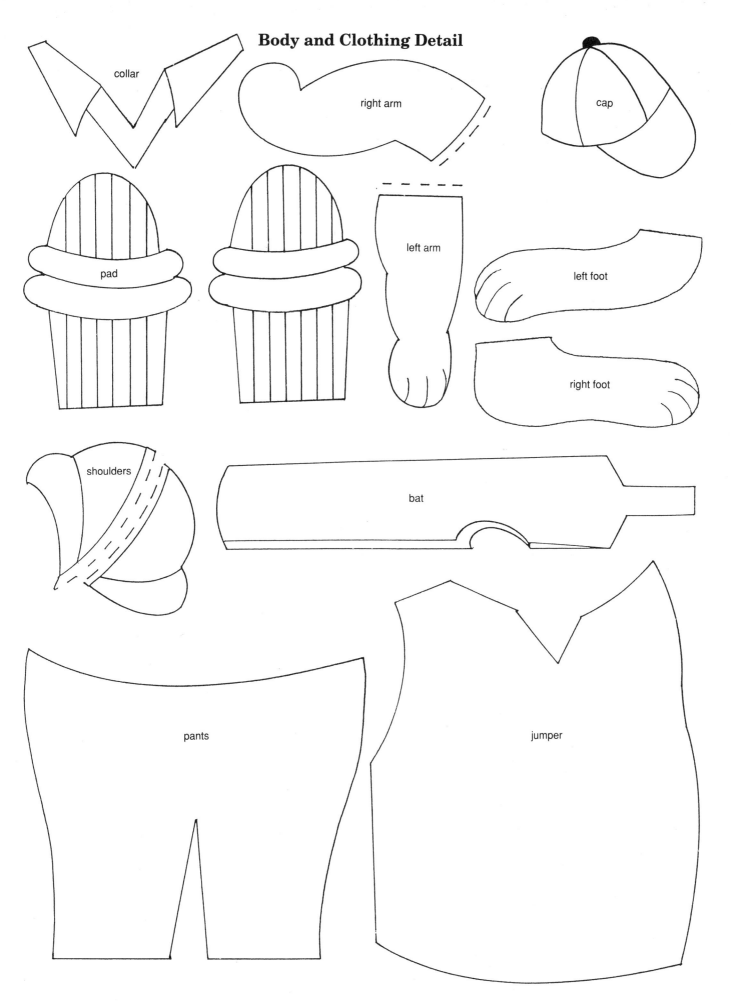

collar

right arm

cap

pad

left arm

left foot

right foot

shoulders

bat

pants

jumper

67

Net and Background Detail

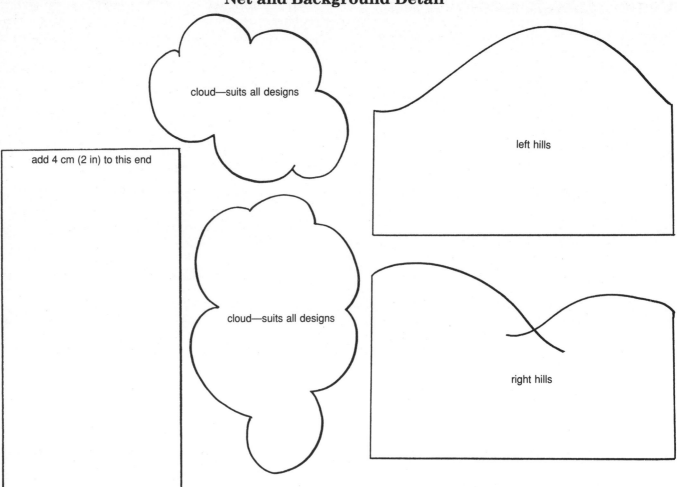

cloud—suits all designs

cloud—suits all designs

left hills

right hills

add 4 cm (2 in) to this end

fence or net—suits all designs

Materials Required

Fabric

Quilt square	30 x 43 cm	(12 x 17 in)
Lime green grass	22 x 32 cm	(9 x 13 in)
sky	23 x 32 cm	(9 x 13 in)
Dark green	8 x 32 cm	(3 x 13 in)
Gold	22 x 22 cm	(9 x 9 in)
Orange	10 x 12 cm	(4 x 5 in)
Royal blue	20 x 24 cm	(8 x 10 in)
White	22 x 26 cm	(9 x 10 in)
Red	6 x 17 cm	(3 x 7 in)
Scrap of hot pink		
Scrap of black		

Satin ribbon   white 50 cm (20 in) each of 2 cm (1 in)
                 and 1 cm (1/2 in)
                 red   50 cm (20 in) each of 1 cm (1/2 in)
                 and 5 mm (1/4 in)

Double-sided iron-on interlining
Dressmaker's carbon, tracing wheel
Unwaxed greaseproof paper
HB pencil
Cotton thread to match or highlight
Black embroidery thread

Construction Procedure

Trace and cut out your pattern pieces. Place these onto your fabric and measure out approximate squares of each colour.

Cut out similar squares of your double-sided iron-on interlining slightly smaller so it will not stick to your ironing board or iron.

Turn your fabric wrong side up and place your interlining over the material squares, paper upwards, sticky side to the material, making sure there is no overhang to stick to the ironing board. Press with a dry iron.

Place your pattern pieces mirror-reverse onto the paper backing, and trace around your patterns. Now cut these out.

For those making the quilt: Each square is 31 x 44 cm (12 x 16 in). After pressing your iron-on interlining to your lime green grass, sky and dark green hills, remove the backing and press to the quilt backing fabric. Use a lightweight dress material, light in colour with no design. Leave the clouds until the lion is in position.

Lay your background pieces onto your background fabric. When in position, peel off the protective paper and steam press.

Before you can start to assemble your lion, you will need to stitch the satin ribbons to the jumper. By placing a piece of greaseproof paper behind your blue jumper and also leaving the paper backing from the iron-on interlining, you can stitch on the ribbons without trouble.

Once they are in position and stitched, you may then start to assemble your lion design. Remove the greaseproof paper from the jumper but do not remove the backing paper until you are happy with your design.

To assemble, slide the orange face under the gold mane and slide both under the white collar. Slide the blue jumper under the collar but over the sleeves. The white pants should be under the blue jumper with the blue pads over them. The feet and arms go under the legs of the trousers, and also the white sleeves. Place the red bat under the right paw with the ball not far from the base of the bat.

Place the ear and inner ear into position and the eyes into place with the nose just under the eyes. The hot pink tongue must be trimmed so it sits right on the line that you will stitch in orange with the black tongue sliding under the hot pink tongue in a similar manner. Now place the cap on an angle tilted over the right ear. Place the clouds in position.

When you are happy with the design, gently peel off the protective backing and, making sure the position has not changed, place unwaxed greaseproof paper over the design. Turn your iron to steam and press down one section at a time. Do not glide the iron over the design until it is all adhered to the background fabric.

Place unwaxed greaseproof paper behind your background fabric and prepare your machine for stitching.

Stitching Procedure

Thread your machine with gold cotton and wind your bobbin with the same colour unless you intend to use a white bobbin for all colours. (If you set your tension at 3, the white will not show through.)

Start at the right-hand side (RHS) of the lion's head nearest the cap. Adjust your stitch width to 1 1/2, quickly increasing it to 3 and then reducing it as you come around the curves of the mane. When you reach the ear, secure thread and start on the other side finishing at the cap. Secure thread.

Now, do the inside face in the same cotton, reducing at the peaks of the mane in the same manner as before. Now, do the outer ear starting at the bottom of the ear, secure thread and stitch around the curve remembering to pivot so the curve is nicely rounded and then back to the straight section. Pivot and return to the start.

Starting at the right arm just under the white sleeve, secure thread and stitch around the paw and back again. Reduce your stitch width to 2 and do the lines inside the paw. Secure thread and start on the left arm and paw, the arm closest to the jumper, and finishing at the outside cuff. Secure thread.

Secure thread and start on the right foot, remembering to pivot as you go around the foot and back to the end. Do the inside lines after you have completed the left foot by reducing the stitch width down to 2.

Change to blue and use the slow button, if you have one, and set your stitch width at 3 1/2. Stitch the edge of the jumper. Because you are going to go over the ends of the ribbons you will either have to go very slowly to enable your machine to get more stitches in to cover the ribbon or you will need to go over the line twice.

When you get to the bottom of the jumper, pivot and go across to the left paw, secure and do the armhole and shoulder as before.

Reduce your stitch width back to 3 and start on your cap. Starting on the inside line of the cap brim go around the curve, pivot at mane and around the top of the hat back down to the brim and finally merging into the centre line. Now do the internal lines of the hat. If you are going to stitch the button in, adjust the stitch width to 3 1/2 and hold your fabric so you can oversew. Either that or embroider it later or sew a small covered button in place.

With the leg pads, start by doing the two centre sections first, remembering to reduce your stitch width to 2 and pivot at the curves. Secure thread and now adjust back to 3 and do the outside edges finishing up by doing the straight internal lines at a stitch width of 2. Secure at each end of line. Repeat for both pads. Complete the blue by doing the ball as for instructions on circles in front section of book. (See page 8)

Change to white cotton. Start on the collar doing the curved section first, reducing width as you reach the peak, pivot and stitch back to the shoulder section, coming back down to reach the start. Do the left collar in the same manner. Now do the V lines of the shirt.

For the sleeves, do the cuffs first by starting at the line closest to the arm, coming around the curve and back to the jumper. Secure thread and start at the shoulder and stitch down until you reach the curve. Repeat the same for the left sleeve. now start on the right-hand side (RHS) of the pants pivoting at the edge of the leg and then come across the bottom of the leg. Pivot and back up to the inside leg reducing the stitch width as you reach the top of the inside leg. Repeat the same for the left leg.

Start at the bottom of the clouds remembering to pivot around the curves. Change to your appliqué foot and do the white eyes.

Change to red cotton and start on the outside of the bat. Reduce your stitch width for the first few stitches after securing your thread and then increase the width to 3. Stitch down until you reach the angle section of the bat. Pivot and do the angle. Pivot and come down to the hole in the bat. Pivot as for the circle instructions (see page 8) until you come to the edge. Pivot and go straight down to the curved base. Pivot and do the curve. Pivot again and come back up the inside line as for the previous side.

Change to hot pink cotton and do the tongue. Change to black and do the outer tongue, remembering to secure at each end. Do the inner ear, secure thread. Start the nose at the tip pivoting at each corner and back to the tip.

For those who are going to stitch the pupil in by machine, do the curved outline first and fill it in with various lengths until you have completely filled in the pupil. If you intend to embroider it, outline it in stem stitch and use satin stitch for the inside.

The last thing you have to do is to change to a light coloured green for the background hills. If you are doing the design for a quilt, leave approximately 1/2 inch at the edges for seams.

AMERICAN BALD EAGLE BASEBALL PLAYER

Materials Required

Fabric

Quilt square	30 x 43 cm	(12 x 17 in)
Lime green grass	22 x 32 cm	(9 x 13 in)
Sky	26 x 32 cm	(10 x 13 in)
Black/white fence	8 x 32 cm	(3 x 13 in)
Red	22 x 22 cm	(9 x 9 in)
White	13 x 22 cm	(5 x 9 in)
Royal blue	13 x 17 cm	(5 x 7 in)
Brown	14 x 18 cm	(6 x 7 in)
Yellow	8 x 22 cm	(3 x 9 in)
White cloud	10 x 14 cm	(4 x 6 in)

Double-sided iron-on interlining
Dressmaker's carbon, tracing wheel
Unwaxed greaseproof paper
HB pencil
Cotton thread to match or highlight
Black embroidery thread

American Bald Eagle
Baseball Player Master Design

Arm, Foot and Equipment Detail

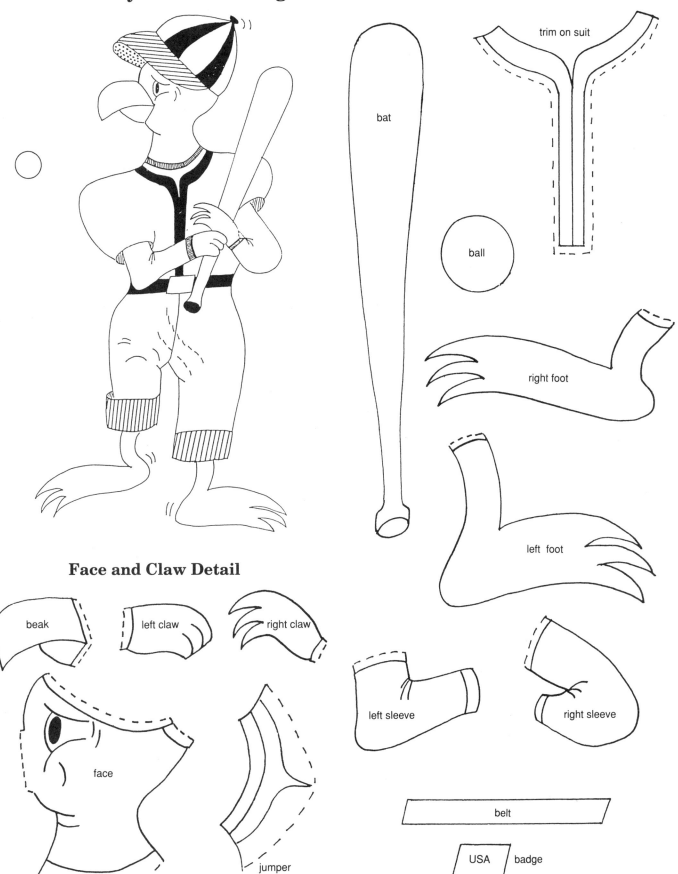

bat

trim on suit

ball

right foot

left foot

left sleeve

right sleeve

belt

USA   badge

Face and Claw Detail

beak

left claw

right claw

face

jumper

Clothing Detail

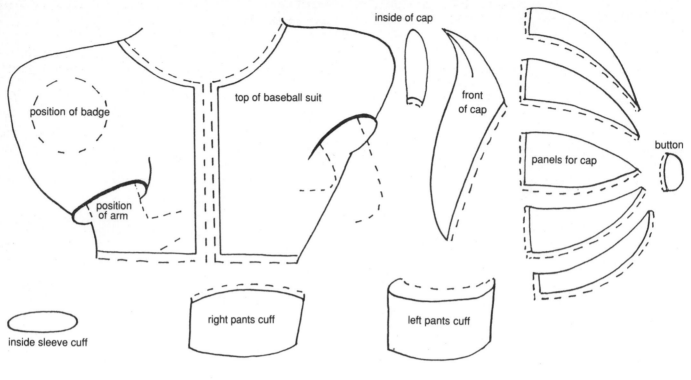

inside of cap

top of baseball suit

position of badge

front of cap

panels for cap

button

position of arm

inside sleeve cuff

right pants cuff

left pants cuff

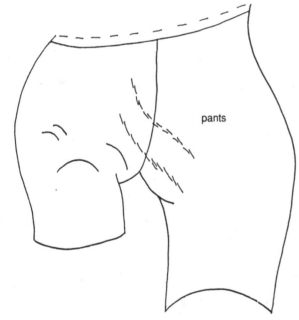

pants

Construction Procedure

Trace and cut out your pattern pieces. Place these onto your fabrics and measure out approximate squares of each colour.

Cut out similar squares of your double-sided iron-on interlining slightly smaller so it will not stick to your ironing board or iron.

Turn your fabric wrong side up and place your interfacing over the material squares, paper upwards, sticky side to the material, making sure there is no overhang to stick to the ironing board. Press with a dry iron.

Place your pattern pieces mirror-reverse onto the paper backing, and trace around the pattern. Now cut these out.

Now, lay out your fabric and place the green grass on to it together with the fence and sky. When happy with their position, peel off the paper backing and press down with a steam iron.

Start to place the sections of the baseball player into position. Again, when you are happy with the position, very carefully, peel off the protective backing paper. The design is fiddly so you may find it helpful to place sections like the hat with tweezers.

First place the cloud, then the red suit, getting your position. Then add the face and blue jumper, cuffs, feet, etc. Place the bat under the claws and the belt under the bat. Once you have the position of the suit, bat, arms, and claws, etc. correctly placed, carefully peel off the paper and press with a steam iron. Do not slide the iron. Lift and hold down until the design adheres to the background fabric. Leave the hat until last. You can press everything else before you attempt the hat. These sections are the fiddly parts.

Lay the red over the white and the blue over the red pieces and the button over all pieces. The red brim is placed over the coloured sections with the blue under-brim under the red. When in position, steam press in the same manner until the entire design adheres to the background fabric. Don't forget the ball.

Place unwaxed greaseproof paper behind your background fabric and prepare your machine for stitching.

Stitching Procedure

Thread your machine with red cotton and wind your bobbin with the same colour, unless you intend to use a white bobbin for all colours. (If you set your tension at 3, the white will not show through.)

Set your stitch width at 3 to 3 1/4 and your length at 1/2. Attach your appliqué or embroidery foot. Adjust your pressure dial.

Working on the right-hand side (RHS) of the design start at the right shoulder, secure thread and stitch around the shoulder until you reach the bat. Secure before and after the bat, finishing at the blue arm. Pivot and stitch across the top of the blue arm, reducing your stitch as you reach the inside arm nearest the claw. Now, do an identical row above that row as per the pattern.

Stitch the small sections of red between the blue arm and the brown claw, remembering to secure thread. Now stitch the section between the arm and belt.

Secure thread and start pants under the belt, working your way around them until you reach the creases in the pants. Secure thread and do the curve in the pants at the crutch. Go back to the belt and do the middle seam from the belt to the crutch, bringing the curve around to join the second leg. Secure thread and finish the left leg. Secure thread and then do the crease marks, remembering to secure thread before and after each one.

Start on the left arm, stitching the two lines above the blue arm as in the RHS. Start with a reduced width of 2 increasing back to 3 as you reach the edge of the red sleeve. Complete the shoulder and the inside line of the sleeve.

You now need to stitch the red sections of the hat. Starting at the base, secure thread, and reduce stitch width as you reach the top of the hat. Do only the top section of the red insert as the bottom section will be stitched in blue.

Now, start at the base of the hat. Do the curved section of the brim reducing slightly as you reach the peak. Pivot and come back around the remainder of the red brim and secure thread. For those who wish to appliqué the button reduce your width to 2. You may need to go over this twice to tidy it up as it is a difficult small circumference. As an alternative, you could sew on a small button.

Now stitch the ball, remembering to pivot regularly so as to form a perfect circle. Then do movement lines at ball, head and feet.

Change to blue and start on the right arm, stitching around the wrist and into the crease of the arm, reducing your stitch width. Stitch the two creases and continue back up to the red arm. Repeat the same for the left arm. Do the two cuffs on pants and belt, remembering to secure thread on either side of the buckle.

Stitch the blue neckline of the jumper, and now the blue section of the hat on both sides. Then do the inside of the brim. When doing the blue section of the hat, you will need to reduce your stitch width to merge into the red button, being careful not to sew over the red.

Change to brown cotton and do the claws, starting at the bottom side of the right claw, reducing your stitch width, as you reach the tips of the claws. Now complete the second claw.

Starting on the right foot, stitch until you reach the ankle. Pivot and do the top of the foot reducing your stitch as you do each claw. Reduce your stitch width as you reach the inside of the claw. Continue back around until you reach the blue cuff. Repeat same for left foot.

Change to yellow thread, and do the beak, starting on the centre line first and reducing at the tip of beak. Pivot and come around the top until you reach the forehead. Pivot and stitch until you reach the centre line. Pivot and complete the beak. Secure thread.

Starting on the side of the bat that is closest to the face, secure thread above claw and continue around until you reach the claw again, remembering to pivot regularly at the curve at the top of the bat. If there is any yellow showing through between the claws do that and secure thread. Now start on the RHS of the handle working your way around to the claw. Now do the eye and the eye expressions.

Change to black and do the fence. If you are making the design into a quilt, do not take the stitching right to the edge but leave about 1/2 inch. Secure. Complete the white cloud. Pivot around the curves and secure thread.

For the pupil of the eye, either start by reducing your width to 2 and quickly increase it up to about 4 and back down again. If hand-embroidering, use an outline stitch and satin stitch the inside.

AUSTRALIAN KOALA BASKETBALL PLAYER

Australian Koala
Basketball Player Master Design

BASKETBALL

Materials Required

Fabric

Quilt square	30 x 43 cm	(12 x 17 in)
Grey	25 x 25 cm	(10 x 10 in)
Gold	14 x 16 cm	(6 x 6 in)
Green	10 x 14 cm	(4 x 6 in)
Red	7 x 7 cm	(3 x 3 in)
Blue	10 x 22 cm	(4 x 9 in)
Black mesh	3 x 3 cm	(1 x 1 in)
Black	14 x 14 cm	(5 x 5 in)
Brown	6 x 6 cm	(3 x 3 in)
White	10 x 20 cm	(4 x 8 in)

Double-sided iron-on interlining
Dressmaker's carbon, tracing wheel
Unwaxed greaseproof paper
HB pencil
Cotton thread to match or highlight

Head and Face Detail

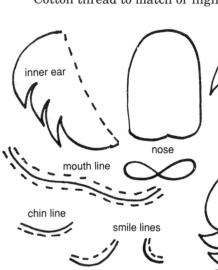

74

Body and Clothing Detail

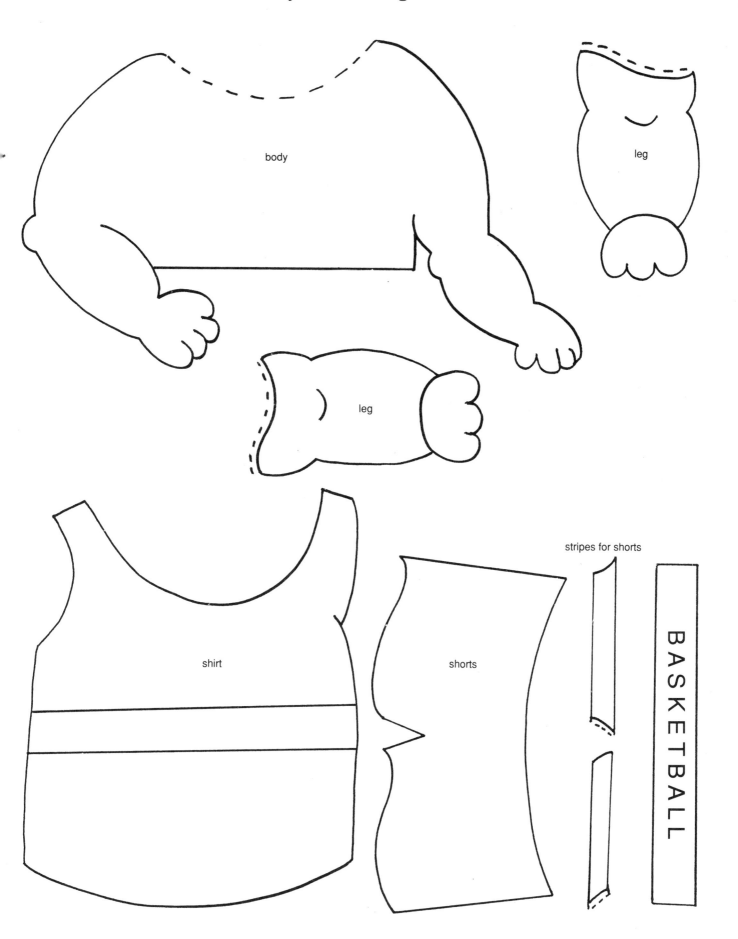

body

leg

leg

shirt

shorts

stripes for shorts

BASKETBALL

75

Equipment Detail

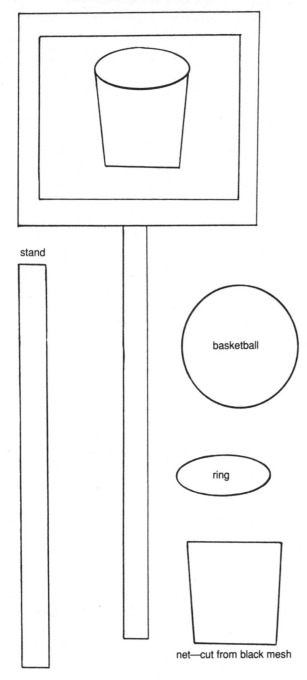

stand

basketball

ring

net—cut from black mesh

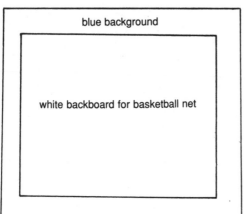

blue background

white backboard for basketball net

Construction Procedure

Measure out required amounts of fabric. Mark out your pattern pieces and cut approximate squares of each colour.

Cut out similar squares of your double-sided iron-on interlining slightly smaller so it will not stick to your ironing board or iron.

Turn your fabric wrong side up and place your interlining over the material squares, paper upwards, sticky side to the material, making sure there is no overhang to stick to the ironing board. Press with a dry iron.

Place your pattern pieces, mirror-reverse onto the paper backing, and trace around your patterns. Now cut these out.

Using a hard surface and your HB pencil or dressmaker's carbon, trace the facial lines of the koala. Place the nose and eyes into position first. Pencil in a light line where they will go and then draw in darker pencil the facial lines and the knees.

For those making the quilt: After pressing your iron-on interlining to your lime green grass, blue sky and red and white striped fence, remove the paper backing and press to the quilt backing fabric. Use a lightweight dress material light in colour with no design. Leave the cloud until you have positioned the basketball net.

Place the head, legs, singlet, and shorts into position on the background fabric. Once you have decided on the position of your design, remove the paper backing from the head and put back into position.

Now, remove the backing from the shoulders and arms and place under the head. To get the singlet to fit under the arms, you need to cut a small slit up the arm. Now, place the singlet under the arm but over the shoulders and neck. Remove the backing from the shorts and place them under the singlet and place the legs under the shorts. The angle you place the legs determines whether he is running or standing.

Now, remove the backing from the black inner ears and slide them under the face.

Now, remove the backing from the shirt stripes and place them under the arm. Then do the gold stripes on the shorts. Slide them under the singlet.

Check that everything is in position. Place unwaxed greaseproof paper over the design and using a steam iron press down in one downward motion. Lift and press another section. Do not slide your iron over your design until it is completely adhered to the background fabric.

Now place the nose, eyes, and headband into position and press. Remove the backing from the blue background for the basketball net and then place the white over it. Lastly, making sure the mesh is well covered by the black, place them into position and press. Place cloud into position. Remove paper and steam press. Now remove the backing from the ball and press in the same manner as before.

Place unwaxed greaseproof paper behind your background fabric and prepare your machine for stitching.

Stitching Procedure

Thread your machine with grey cotton and wind your bobbin with the same colour, unless you intend to use a white bobbin for all colours. (If you set your tension at 3, the white will not show through.)

Secure thread and set your width at 3 to 3 1/4 and start just below the peaks of the hair. For the face, use your slow button, if you have one, and go very carefully over the black. You need to cover the black in one go. If you go over it, it makes the face stand out and spoils the balance of the design.

Follow the face around and pivot at the peaks of the hair. Reduce at the ends and secure thread at the inside ends.

Now start on the right ear. Reduce at the outside of the peak. Pivot at each one, and secure at face. Repeat the same for the left ear.

Come down to the right arm and pivot around the paw and the elbow. Secure thread. For the left arm start at the inside line opposite elbow. Secure thread and come across the singlet and around the paw, pivot and come back up. Pivot at the elbow. Secure thread.

Do the legs before the feet. Stitch all four sides of the legs and secure at each end. For the paw, start at the inside curve of the right paw closest to the middle. Secure thread and come around the outside curve. Pivot where necessary. Now, come around the top of the paw and back down around the two remaining curves in the same manner. Repeat the same for the left paw. Now stitch in the knee and the facial lines, taking care to follow your pencil lines exactly.

Now change to gold thread and start at the left-hand side (LHS) of the singlet. Turn your design upside down and start nearest the arm. Secure thread and stop at the shoulders and pivot and come around the neckline. Go slowly so your stitching will come around in a nice curve. Pivot at the shoulders and back down the right-hand side (RHS) of singlet. Pivot at corner and come across the bottom, pivot and come back up the LHS. Secure

thread. Go slowly over the green stripes to get good coverage.

For the headband, insert your needle right up close to the grey stitching. Secure thread and complete. Secure thread.

Complete the stripes on shorts, but stop a few stitches short of the end at the bottom to allow the green stitching to cover the stripe. Change to green for the shorts and stripes. Secure at each end of the stripes.

Change to black and do the inner ears in the same manner as the outer ears. For the nose complete the nostrils first in a figure 8 and secure. Now, complete the nose. Secure thread and start at the LHS coming around to the RHS.

Now, do the pupils. Reduce your width slightly and start just below where the brown stitching will go. Secure thread and come down to the bottom line, stopping just on that line where the stitching will go. Secure thread.

Making sure the mesh is fully enclosed under the black ring of the net, secure thread and do the ring. Pivot regularly where necessary and secure thread. Then, outline the mesh taking care to fully encase it.

Change to brown for the eyes. (I always use a lighter shade than the fabric.) Reduce your stitch width to 1/2 and secure thread. Increase your width to 3 1/2 in the middle of the eye and back down again as you reach the corners. Pivot and repeat same for the bottom line and the left eye.

Now, change to blue and outline the basketball net board and also the white outline. Now, complete the white cloud. Pivot around curves and secure. Change to red and pivot regularly around the ball. Secure thread. Now, complete top and bottom of red fence. Secure thread at each side of koala and basketball net board. Leave a 1 cm (1/2 in) trim at the ends if you are making the quilt.

AMERICAN RACCOON GOLF PLAYER

Face and Upper Body Details

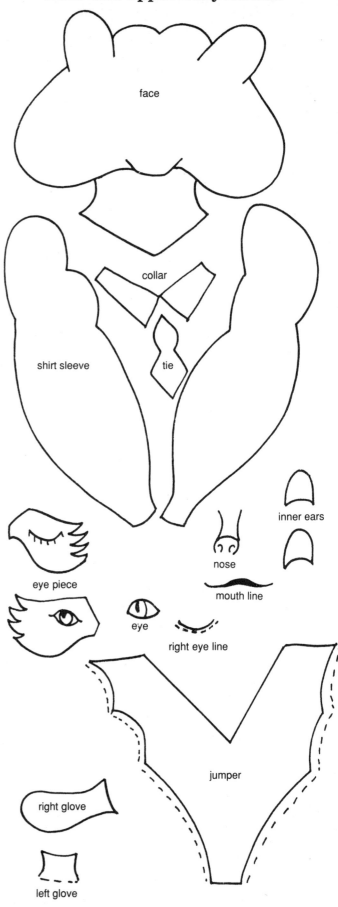

face

collar

shirt sleeve

tie

inner ears

eye piece

nose

mouth line

eye

right eye line

jumper

right glove

left glove

American Raccoon Golf Player Master Design

Lower Body and Background Details

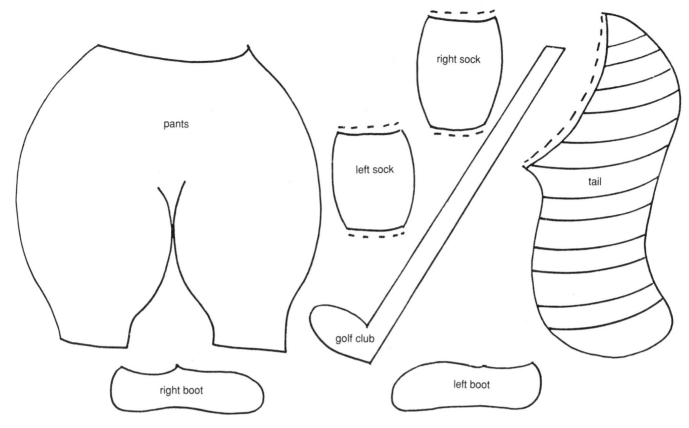

pants

right sock

left sock

tail

golf club

right boot

left boot

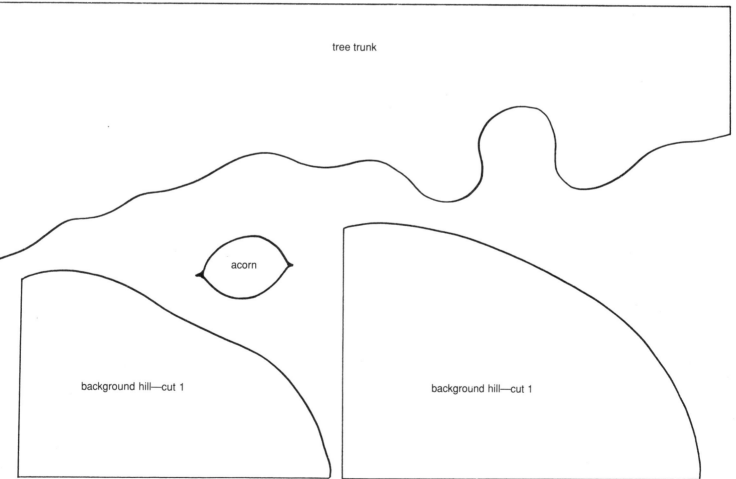

tree trunk

acorn

background hill—cut 1

background hill—cut 1

Tree Top Detail

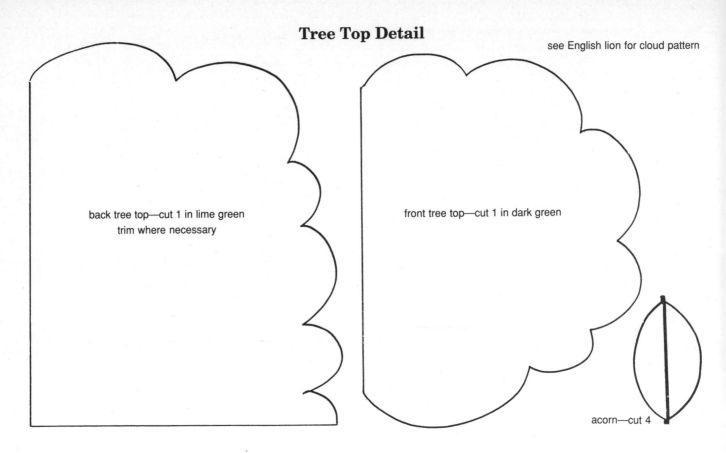

back tree top—cut 1 in lime green
trim where necessary

see English lion for cloud pattern

front tree top—cut 1 in dark green

acorn—cut 4

Materials Required

Fabric

Quilt square	30 x 43 cm	(12 x 17 in)
Grey	10 x 20 cm	(4 x 8 in)
Tartan	12 x 12 cm	(5 x 5 in)
White	14 x 18 cm	(6 x 7 in)
Red	10 x 10 cm	(4 x 4 in)
Black	10 x 10 cm	(4 x 4 in)
Blue	2 x 4 cm	(1 x 2 in)
Brown	4 x 25 cm	(2 x 10 in)
Dark green	25 x 30 cm	(10 x 12 in)
Lime green	20 x 30 cm	(8 x 12 in)
Blue (sky)	25 x 30 cm	(10 x 12 in)
Bone	10 x 10 cm	(4 x 4 in)
Yellow	4 x 17 cm	(2 x 7 in)

Double-sided iron-on interlining
Dressmaker's carbon, tracing wheel
Unwaxed greaseproof paper
HB pencil
Cotton thread to match or highlight

Construction Procedure

Measure out required amounts of fabric. Mark out your pattern pieces and cut approximate squares of each colour.

Cut out similar squares of your double-sided iron-on interlining slightly smaller so it will not stick to your ironing board or iron.

Turn your fabric wrong side up, place your interlining over the material squares, paper upwards, sticky side to the material, making sure there is no overhang to stick to the ironing board. Press with a dry iron.

Place your pattern pieces, mirror-reverse onto the paper backing, and trace around your patterns. Now cut these out.

Using a hard surface and your HB pencil or dressmaker's carbon, trace in the facial lines of the nose and mouth. For the eye line on the black, you will need to use a light coloured pencil or dressmaker's chalk.

Lay out your background design first. Once you have ascertained the position, peel off the protective paper backing and reposition. You can now steam press the grass and hills into place. Now, place the tree trunk and top of tree into position. When correct, you can also steam press them. Leave the cloud.

Now, lay out your raccoon and get the approximate position. Now, remove the paper backing from the head and place the head about halfway down the tree top. Now remove backing from white shirt and place collar over the neck. Now, place the red vest over the neck and place the white arms over the red vest making sure that you leave only enough overlap for the stitching to cover. Do not make a large overlap or it will show through the white. If you find that you have too much, lift the arms and trim back the red.

International Stars of Sport Wall-hanging (see page 62).

Australian Gumnuts (see page 85).

Left: Bozo the Clown (see page 88); *right*: Clown Face from Girl's Quilt (see page 28).

Lady's Face (see page 92).

Appliqué Abstract (see page 94).

Now, remove the backing from the pants and slide them under the arms. Then place the white socks under the bottom of the pants. Remove the backing from the tail and slide it under the edge of the pants and arm.

Now, remove the backing from the golf stick and place it between the two arms. Remove the backing from the gloves and place the left glove under the golf stick and the right glove over the stick. Now, place the tie into position. Remove the backing from the shoes and place them over the socks.

Now, remove the backing from the black eye sections and place them right up on the edge of the nose. Leave just enough room for you to stitch and to have a very small gap between. Now, place the white inner ears and check that all is in place.

Place unwaxed greaseproof paper over the design and press down with a steam iron. Now remove the backing from the eye and place into position and press. Now remove the backing from the dark brown section of the nuts and place into position. Now place the light brown section of the nut under the dark brown. Now steam press again. Lift iron and hold it down until the design completely adheres to the fabric background. Place cloud in position. Remove the backing paper and steam press.

Stitching Procedure

Thread your machine with grey thread, and wind your bobbin with the same colour, unless you intend to use a white bobbin for all colours. (If you set your tension at 3, the white will not show through.)

Set your stitch width at 3 and start at the top part of the right ear. Secure and pivot around the ear. Pivot at corner and come around the cheek and stop at chin. Secure thread and do the chin. Secure thread and come down to the start of the left cheek. Come back up the left cheek and pivot around the ear. Pivot at edge of ear and in the middle of head, secure thread at right ear.

Now do the neck sections. Come down and start at the tail. Start at the right-hand side (RHS) nearest the arm and come down around until you join up with the pants. Secure thread.

Change to white and secure thread and stitch the small section of shoulder. Secure thread and complete the collar. Start at the bottom edge of the collar nearest the shoulder. Secure thread close to the stitching and pivot at the corner of collar, and back to the shoulder. Secure thread and repeat same for left-hand side (LHS).

For the arms start at the top edge on the outside line of the arm, secure thread and pivot round the curves and finish at the glove. Secure thread and go to the inner line. Secure thread and come back up the arm stopping about 3/4 of an inch from the top of the arm. (Do this in red later).

Now complete the socks, securing at each end. Then go to the inner ears and secure thread at the right ear. Start at the top RHS and secure and pivot around the curve and back down to the other side. Pivot, come across the straight edge and secure. Leave the eye until later. You can now do the cloud. Pivot around the curves and secure.

Change to red and do the vest. Start at the LHS, where you left the white stitching and secure thread and come up the arm, across the shoulder and down the V and the same for the RHS.

For the gloves, start at the top edge of the glove closest to the middle. Secure and pivot at corners and around the curve and back to the start and secure. For the left glove, start at the bottom line nearest the club and secure thread and complete the glove. Change to yellow and start just below the right glove. Secure and come down the club around the curve. Pivot where necessary and come back up the LHS of the club. Reduce your stitch width down to fit in between the two gloves and then increase it to finish.

Change to black and starting at the right boot, secure thread and come across the top of the boot around the curve. Pivot where necessary and come back across and back to the start. Secure thread, and repeat the same for the LHS.

Now, follow the pencil lines of the tail. Secure thread and carefully stitch on those lines. Do not go over the grey stitching.

For the outer eyes, reduce your stitch width down to approximately 2 1/2 and carefully stitch the peaks of the eyes. Reduce at each end of the peak and come back to the start. Repeat the same for the LHS.

Now, change to blue and slightly increase your stitch width back up and do the tie. Starting at the top, secure thread and pivot around the curve stopping at vest. Secure and repeat for other side. Now, starting at the RHS of the pants, secure thread, come down to bottom of pants, pivot and come across the bottom edge. Pivot and go back up to the curve at top of legs. Secure thread and repeat same for the LHS.

Change to brown and do the tree trunk. Pivot around the hole in trunk. Now do the top part of the nuts. Do 4 to 5 stitches at edge of nut before you start the nut and do not cover the centre line in brown, but do it in light brown. Change to dark green and do the hills and tree top and change to lime green and complete the other tree top, pivot at each curve.

Now, change back to black and reduce your stitch width down to 2 or less and do the outline of the nose. Stop at the curve of the nose and do this separately. Reduce the stitch to 1 for the mouth and increase it to approximately 2 in the middle, and back down again. Secure at each end.

For those who wish to hand-embroider, use a stem stitch for the outline of the nose, and a very small satin stitch for the curved section of the nose. Use a small satin stitch also for the nose, gradually increasing it towards the middle, and back down again at edge of the mouth.

Now change back to white for the eye. Follow the curve line for the RHS, and secure at each end. For the left eye, reduce the stitch width down to 1/2 and secure thread. Increase it back up to approximately 2 towards the middle and decrease it back down at the corner of the eye. Secure thread, and come back across the bottom of the eye in the same manner. Start at the bottom of the cloud, remembering to pivot around the curves.

For the pupil, use a fine stem stitch to outline the pupil and satin stitch for the centre of pupil.

Materials Required

Fabric

Quilt square	30 x 43 cm	(12 x 17 in)
Lime green grass	22 x 32 cm	(9 x 13 in)
Sky	22 x 32 cm	(9 x 13 in)
Red/white	10 x 32 cm	(4 x 13 in)
Gold	20 x 22 cm	(8 x 9 in)
White	20 x 30 cm	(8 x 12 in)
Black	15 x 22 cm	(6 x 9 in)
Royal blue fence	2 x 31 cm	(1 x 12 in)
Red	10 x 12 cm	(4 x 5 in)
Orange	4 x 10 cm	(2 x 4 in)
Scrap of black		

Double-sided iron-on interlining
Dressmaker's carbon, tracing wheel
Unwaxed greaseproof paper/backing paper
HB pencil
Cotton thread to match or highlight
Black embroidery cotton

New Zealand Kiwi Football Player Master Design

NEW ZEALAND KIWI FOOTBALL PLAYER

Head and Limb Detail

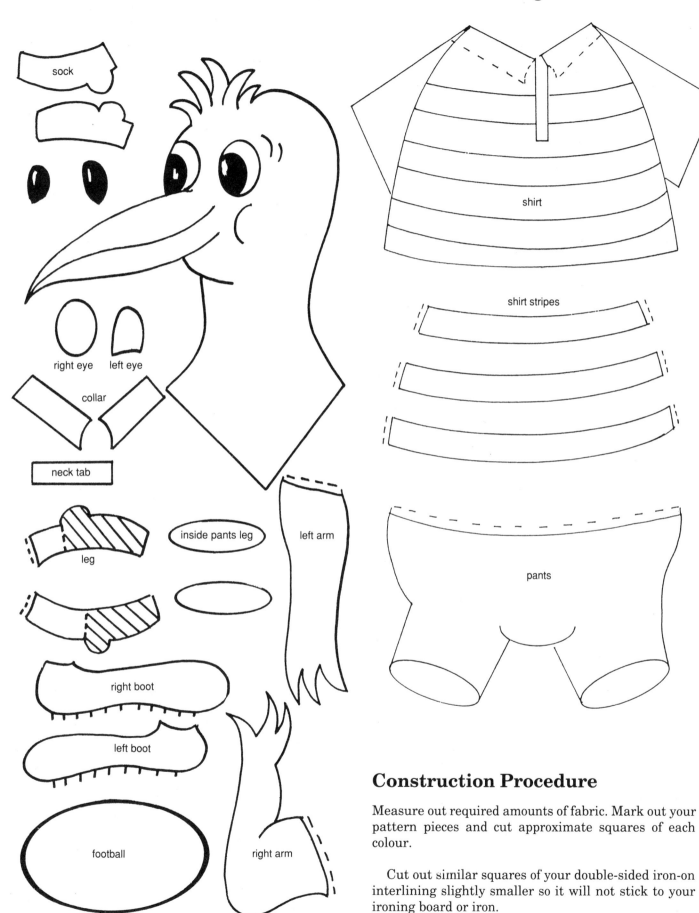

sock

right eye   left eye

collar

neck tab

leg

inside pants leg

left arm

right boot

left boot

football

right arm

Clothing Detail

shirt

shirt stripes

pants

Construction Procedure

Measure out required amounts of fabric. Mark out your pattern pieces and cut approximate squares of each colour.

Cut out similar squares of your double-sided iron-on interlining slightly smaller so it will not stick to your ironing board or iron.

Turn your fabric wrong side up and place your inter-lining over the material squares, paper upwards, sticky side to the material, making sure there is no overhang to stick to the ironing board. Press with a dry iron.

Place your pattern pieces mirror-reverse onto the paper backing, and trace around your patterns. Now, cut these out.

Lay out background pieces on to your background fabric, first laying the fence over the grass and sky. Leave clouds until you have positioned the head.

Place the head of the kiwi so the chin is just above the top edge of the fence, sliding the head under the jumper with both arms under the jumper. Place the shorts over the jumper, but under the right claw. You will need to trim the legs to fit just on the top edge of the red underlining of the pants. Place the white socks over the yellow legs and the red football boots over the white socks. Place the eyes into position as with the football and the clouds.

Once you are happy with the position of your design, carefully peel off the protective paper backing. Place unwaxed greaseproof paper over the design. Check that nothing has moved. Place your steam iron over one part of the design and hold down. Do not slide the iron over the design until you have firmly pressed all the design to the background fabric.

Now mark in all the movement lines in whatever method you choose.

Place unwaxed greaseproof paper behind your fabric background and prepare your machine for stitching.

Stitching Procedure

Thread your machine with orange cotton and wind your bobbin with the same colour unless you intend to use a white bobbin for all colours. (If you set your tension at 3, the white will not show through.)

Starting with orange cotton, secure thread, and do the centre line of the beak, reducing it as you reach the bottom line of the beak. Secure thread, go back to the bottom line of the beak, secure, and stitch down to the top of the beak, reducing stitch width. Pivot and come around the top of the beak, going slowly over the white of the eye (bottom of eye) to ensure that all the white material is covered with the orange stitching. Secure thread and start just above the eye on the left-hand side (LHS).

Stitch until you reach the start of the spiky hair. Pivot and stitch until you reach the tip of the first piece. Reduce as you reach the tip, pivot and return to the

top of the head, reducing again. Pivot and proceed in the same manner until you have completed all the hair pieces.

Stitch around the head until you finish at the collar. Secure thread, and start on the LHS of the collar stitching until you reach the curve of the chin. Secure thread and start at the curve, finishing at the start of the beak.

If you intend to do the facial expressions in the same colour, do these now. With a stitch width of 2 1/2, pivot every few stitches. Secure thread at the start and finish off each one.

Start now at the right arm just below the white sleeve, doing the claws in the same manner as the hair. Complete the left arm in the same manner. For the legs, start on the right leg first but leave a small space to allow the overstitching of the red and the same for the left leg.

Change to black and do the stripes of the jumper, remembering to leave a few stitches at the end to allow for the overstitching of the sides of the jumper which you will do after you have done the stripes. You may need to go over the side seams twice to completely cover the white fabric. You may also find that slightly widening your stitch width may give you a better coverage.

For the black collar start at the RHS of the curve, reducing the stitch width as you reach the peak. Pivot and return to the shoulder, pivot and go across the shoulder, pivot and back to the start. Repeat the same procedure for the left collar.

Now, start on the shorts, just below the right claw. You may need to slightly reduce your stitch again to get in close, but increase it after a few stitches. Stitch down to the red inner leg, leaving a few stitches for the red overstitching later. Secure thread and start on the other side of the leg until you reach the curve of the pants. Secure thread, and do the curve. Secure thread at both ends. Complete the left leg as in the right leg.

You will have to reduce your stitch width for the football as you reach the tips of the ball. Start on the inner lines first which you will merge into the outer lines by reduction.

If you are doing the pupil of the eyes by machine, do those now, reducing your stitch to 2 1/2 and you may need to go over it twice. If you intend to embroider it, leave it until you have finished your design completely. In whatever method you choose to do the pupils, remember not to oversew where the white will be stitched. It is too hard to cover so leave a few stitches.

Change to white and do the clouds first. Then start on the RHS of the sleeve. Stitch down to the yellow arm, pivot and stitch across the top of the arm and back up to the small section of the underarm. For the left arm you would start at the edge of the jumper and work your way up to the shoulder.

Now, start on the tab of the jumper at the line closest to the black collar and stitch to the end of the tab. Pivot and stitch across the bottom and back up to the top. Pivot and stitch the last few stitches to come back to the black collar. Now, starting at the bottom of the tab, stitch the few stitches between the two openings and back up to the left black collar, remembering to secure your thread before and after each section.

Starting on the right sock, secure thread and stitch the few stitches before you pivot around the knee cap. Stitch in the same manner as you would a circle. It is a tight circle, so sew slowly, using your slow button, if you have one. Complete the sock and repeat in the same manner for the left sock. Change your stitch width to 2 1/2 for the eyes. Again proceed in the same manner as for circles. (See page 8)

Change to red and stitch the inner legs of the shorts. Start on the inside line of the right leg, remembering to pivot regularly to get around the tight curve and finish back at the outline of the leg. Repeat the same for the left leg. For the boots, start at the outside of the right boot going across the top of the boot. Pivot regularly to produce a neat curve and back around the bottom of the boot in the same manner. Secure thread. Finish movement lines. Change to blue and stitch each side of the fence. Secure thread.

AUSTRALIAN GUMNUTS

Materials Required

Fabric

Cinnamon (nuts)	20 x 20 cm	(8 x 8 in)
Avocado green	14 x 20 cm	(6 x 8 in)
Khaki green	10 x 20 cm	(4 x 8 in)
Orange	8 x 18 cm	(3 x 7 in)
Gold	4 x 12 cm	(2 x 5 in)
Dark brown	16 x 16 cm	(6 x 6 in)
Branch	20 x 25 cm	(8 x 10 in)

Double-sided iron-on interlining
Dressmaker's carbon, tracing wheel
Unwaxed greaseproof paper
HB pencil
Cotton thread to match or highlight

Australian Gumnuts Master Design

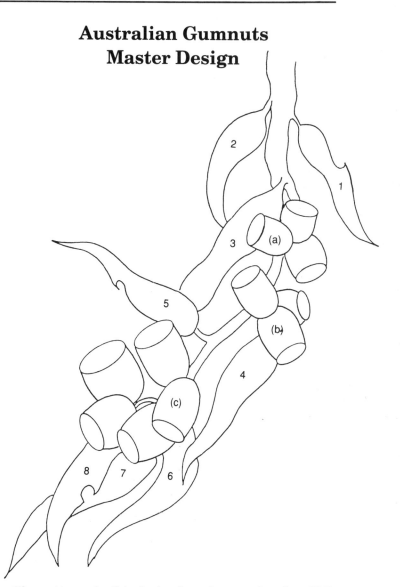

The patterns in this design have been reduced to 75%. See page 10 for instructions on enlarging them to full size.

Leaf and Gumnut Detail

Construction Procedure

Measure out required amounts of fabric. Mark out your pattern pieces and cut approximate squares of each colour.

Cut out similar squares of your double-sided iron-on interlining slightly smaller so it will not stick to your ironing board or iron.

Turn your fabric wrong side up and place your interlining over the material square, paper upwards, sticky side to the material, making sure there is no overhang to stick to the ironing board. Press with a dry iron.

Place your pattern pieces, mirror-reverse onto the paper backing, and trace around your pattern. Now, cut these out.

Using a hard surface and your HB pencil, dressmaker's carbon or cardboard pattern, trace the lines of the gumnuts.

Now, carefully remove the backing from the branch and place into position. Then remove the backing from the large gumnuts and place into position, and then the smaller ones. Now, remove the backing from leaf (4) and slide it under the (b) gumnut. Then remove the backing from leaf (7) and slide it under the gumnuts (c). Then place leaf (8) over (7). Now, place leaf (6) under the gumnuts but over leaf (7). Slide leaf under gumnuts (c) at the top. I have placed leaves (2) and (3) not exactly like the pattern. Try both ways and choose which one appeals to you. Lastly, place leaf (1).

Now, place unwaxed greaseproof paper over the design and press down in one motion. Lift and press down on another section. Repeat until design is completely adhered to background fabric. Now, carefully, one at a time, remove the backing from the dark brown tops of the nuts and place them into position. When correct, place your paper over them and press with a steam iron.

Place unwaxed greaseproof paper behind your background fabric and prepare your machine for stitching.

Stitching Procedure

Thread your machine with chocolate brown cotton for the branch, wind your bobbin with the same colour, unless your intend to use a white bobbin for all colours. (If you set your tension at 3, the white will not show through.)

Now, starting at the end of the leaves (2) and (3) secure thread and come around to the corner, pivot and cross the top, pivot and back around to the front. Work your way down the branch. Stop and secure your thread at the leaf.

Now, change to avocado green for leaves (1), (3), (6), and (8). Proceed with these leaves securing at the start. For those which have the curve cutouts, pivot frequently around them and go slowly. Use your slow button if you have one. Reduce at each tip and pivot and secure at the end of each leaf.

Now, change to a blue/green for the khaki leaves, (I found it gave them a lift) and proceed with leaves (4) and (5).

Now, change to orange and complete leaf (7). Change to gold and complete leaf (2). In this design I have stitched centres down all leaves, reducing at the end of each.

Now, change to cinnamon and starting at gumnut (a) do all the small sections first and the full nuts last. Repeat the same for all gumnuts. Lastly, change your cotton to dark brown and proceed with the inside of the nuts. You will need to pivot frequently. Use your slow button if you have one and secure at ends.

BOZO THE CLOWN

Bozo the Clown Master Design

The patterns in this design have been reduced to 75%. See page 10 for instructions on enlarging them to full size.

Face and Collar Detail

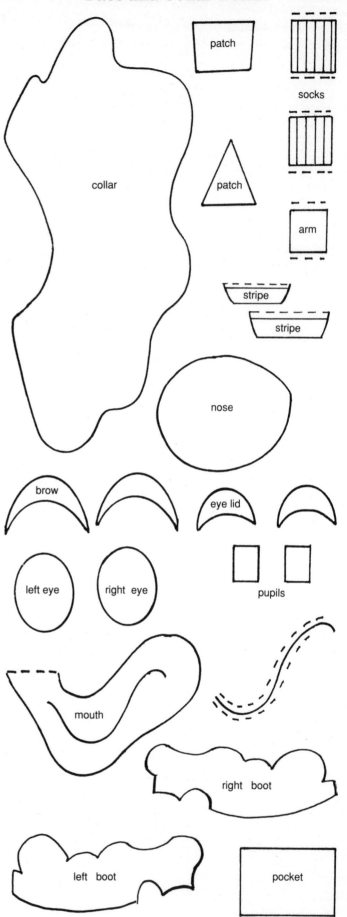

collar

patch

socks

patch

arm

stripe

stripe

nose

brow

eye lid

left eye

right eye

pupils

mouth

right boot

left boot

pocket

Hair and Clothing Detail

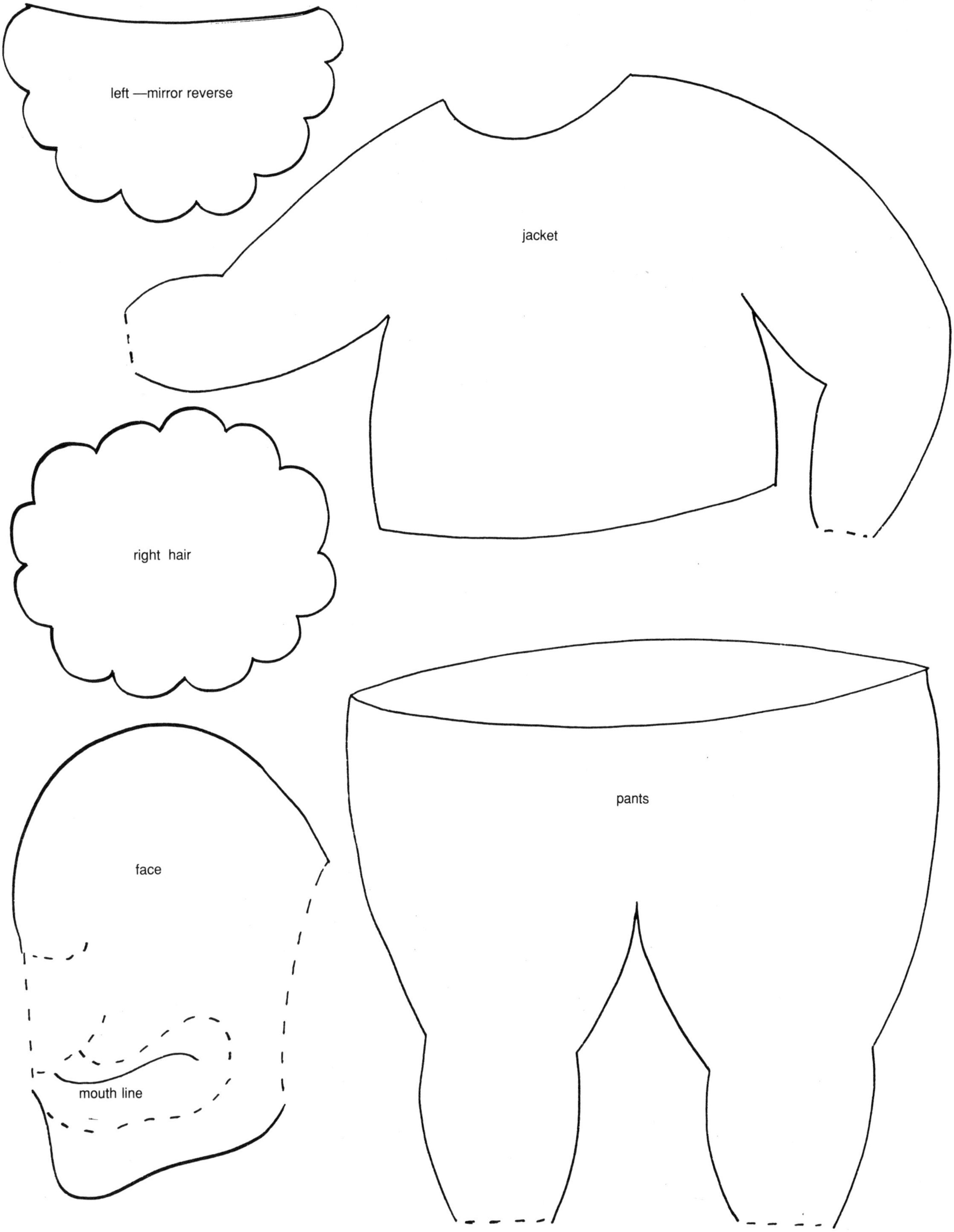

left —mirror reverse

jacket

right hair

face

pants

mouth line

Materials Required

Fabric

Trousers	20 x 20 cm	(8 x	8 in)
Hair	10 x 16 cm	(4 x	6 in)
Boots	4 x 16 cm	(2 x	6 in)
Jacket	13 x 24 cm	(5 x	10 in)
Face	12 x 16 cm	(5 x	7 in)
Hand	5 x 7 cm	(2 x	3 in)
Collar	10 x 18 cm	(4 x	7 in)
Eyebrows	3 x 8 cm	(1 x	3 in)
Nose	6 x 8 cm	(3 x	3 in)
Yellow patch	3 x 3 cm	(1 x	1 in)
Purple patch	3 x 3 cm	(1 x	1 in)
Balloons	6 x 6 cm	(2 x	2 in)
Socks	3 x 4 cm	(1 x	2 in)
Pocket	3 x 8 cm	(1 x	3 in)
Mouth	6 x 8 cm	(3 x	3 in)
Eyelid, pupil	4 x 6 cm	(2 x	3 in)
Eyes	4 x 6 cm	(2 x	3 in)
Stripes	1 x 7 cm	(1/2 x	3 in)

Double-sided iron-on interlining
Dressmaker's carbon, tracing wheel
Unwaxed greaseproof paper
HB pencil
Cotton thread to match or highlight.

Construction Procedure

Measure out required amounts of fabric. Mark out your pattern pieces and cut approximate squares of each colour.

Cut out similar squares of your double-sided iron-on interlining slightly smaller so it will not stick to your ironing board or iron.

Turn your fabric wrong side up and place your interlining over the material square, sticky side down, paper upwards, making sure there is no overhang. Press with a dry iron.

Place your pattern pieces, mirror-reverse onto the paper backing, and trace around your patterns. Now cut these out.

Using a hard surface and your HB pencil or dressmaker's carbon, trace out the facial lines and the extended lines of the trousers. Place the eyes, brows, and nose into position. Lightly mark their position and remove. Now, mark in the two wrinkles under the eye position.

Now, you are ready to lay out your design. Do this by placing the face and body into position. When you have ascertained the correct position, gently remove the paper backing from the shirt and replace it into position. Repeat the same for collar, face, and trousers.

I find it easier to remove the paper backing from the base sections of the design before placing the rest of the design. That way I do not disturb the whole design. When placing the collar, remember to place it well down on the shoulders and the face well down on the collar. If you sit them up high, the clown's head tends to look like a pimple on a pumpkin.

Now, remove the paper backing from the hair and place the left-hand side (LHS) hair under the face, and the right-hand side (RHS) hair halfway between the top of the head and the collar and far enough away from the eye positions. For now, just pat these down with your hand.

Arrange the balloons, under each other after peeling off the paper backing. You can also place the two stripes into position, but slide one just under the other so they will overlap when stitched. Place the pink hand under the sleeve and under the pocket, each with the backing removed.

Remove the backing and place the socks under the trousers and under the boots. Place the patches into position. Hold your hand down on your design; the heat from your hand will hold it sufficiently while you complete laying out the design.

Place the white eyes into position, the brows above and the nose. Now, place the black lids and pupils over the white. If the black lids are not a perfect fit, pick these up and while you still have the paper backing on, trim them. You can now remove the backing and place into position. Remove the backing from brows, place into position and press with hand.

Place mouth into position after you have removed the backing. Remove the backing from nose and slide the other end of mouth end under it. Remove backing from circle and place. Your design is now ready to steam-press.

Check that nothing has moved. Place a sheet of unwaxed greaseproof paper over the design and hold your steam iron down in one position. Lift and hold down in another position. Repeat until you have completely adhered your design to the fabric. Do not slide your iron over the design until you are sure it is completely adhered in all places as it is easy to move the pieces out of position.

Place unwaxed greaseproof paper behind your background fabric and prepare your machine for stitching.

Stitching Procedure

Thread your machine with the colour of the hair and wind your bobbin with the same colour, unless you intend to use white on the bobbin. (If you set your tension at 3, the white will not show through.)

Starting on the right-hand side (RHS) of the hair, secure thread and pivot around each curve. Pivot at the end of each curve, to give a definite curve. Continue in this fashion until you reach the end. Secure thread. Go to the left-hand side (LHS) hair and start under the nose. Secure thread and repeat as for the RHS. While you have the same colour on your machine, complete the coloured balloon making sure the paper backing is under the balloon and the string of the balloon. When stitching strings, place a double thickness of paper or heavy weight interlining behind fabric. Repeat the stitching of string twice. Secure thread.

Change colour for the face, start at the RHS of the face below the hair, coming around to the end at the nose. Secure thread and start at the other side of the nose and finish at the RHS hair. Secure thread and complete the small section of the right hand. Secure thread at each end. Now, go to the left hand holding the balloons. Secure thread and carefully pivot around the fingers. Secure thread.

Change to the colour of the collar, and starting just below the RHS hair, secure thread and slowly come around the curves. If you take it slowly you should not have to pivot. Secure thread when you have reached the LHS. Now, do the internal lines which represent the folds of the collar. Secure thread at start and finish of each line. If you have a yellow patch on the trousers, do this now and secure. Now, complete the yellow balloon as before.

Change colour for trousers, and starting at the curved edge nearest the jacket on the RHS, secure thread and do the small section to the edge of the trousers. Secure thread and come across the edge of trouser top. Pivot at corner and stitch the small section representing the back of the trousers and secure thread. Secure thread at arm edge and come down the RHS of trousers until you reach the blue band. Secure thread and start on the other side of leg. Pivot at join and come back down the left leg. Secure thread at blue band and come back up the leg finishing at the top of the trousers. Complete green balloon.

Change to the colour of shirt and start at the RHS top of jacket. Secure thread and come down the right arm. Secure at edge of stripe and start at the other side of arm. Complete arm, pivot at armpit and down the body edge and secure thread. Now, start at LHS of jacket above trousers. Secure thread and complete arm. Secure thread at stripe. Complete rest of arm and secure thread. Now, complete both pockets and balloon.

Change to the colour of the nose. Secure thread, pivot regularly around the nose and secure thread. Complete the first stripe. Secure thread and, if you have your stripes overlapping, do only three sides of the stripe. If not, do all four and secure thread. Now, complete the socks. Secure thread at each end. Complete the red balloon.

Change to the colour of the eyebrows and place your needle at the narrow end of the right brow. Reduce your stitch width to 1/2, secure thread, and stitch approximately 2 to 3 stitches. Then gradually increase until you come back to a stitch width of 2 3/4 at the centre of brow, then gradually decrease down to 1/2 at the end. Pivot and repeat the same for the bottom line of brow. Repeat same for left brow. Now, complete the stripe on the sleeve and the trousers.

Now, go to the boots, secure thread and start with your needle inserted right up against the red of the socks. Pivot regularly around the curves at the top of the boot and the small straight section at the front of the boot. Now, come across the straight section of the sole and carefully pivot around the arch and then the heel. Repeat the same for the left boot and secure at end. Complete the blue balloon.

Now, change to the colour of the triangle patch and complete that. Complete balloon if the same colour. Secure thread.

Change to black and adjust your stitch width to 2 3/4 for the outline of the eye. Secure thread, and pivot regularly around the eye. Now, starting just inside that outline, do the line of the eyelid. For this particular clown I stitched the eye in white, thereby making it necessary to reduce the stitch width of the eyelid at each end, as with the eyebrows.

Clown's eyes can be done all in black or as I have done this one. If you choose to do the entire eye in black, do not reduce at the ends of the eyelid.

Now, stitch the outline of the mouth. Reduce the width slightly for the inside line and secure thread at end. Leaving your stitch width the same, complete the wrinkles and secure thread at each end. Increase width to 4 for the braces and secure at end.

I have used a triple stitch for the stitching of the patches in uneven lengths and at different angles for a ragamuffin effect.

LADY'S FACE

Face and Clothing Detail

Lady's Face Master Design

The patterns in this design have been reduced to 75%. See page 10 for instructions on enlarging them to full size.

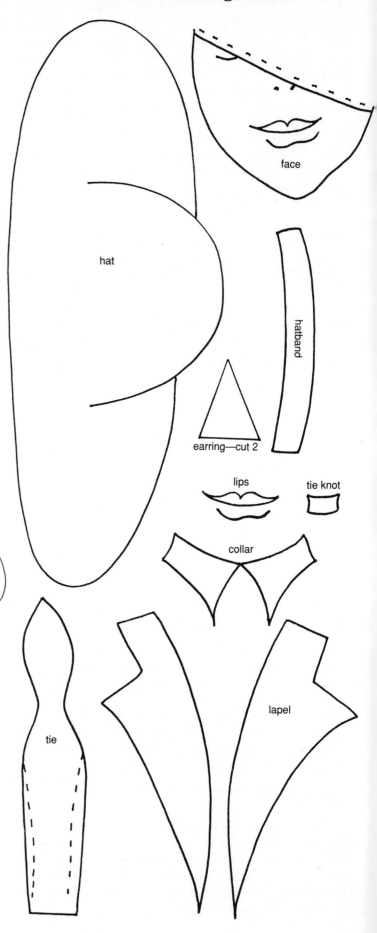

hat

hatband

face

earring—cut 2

lips

tie knot

collar

tie

lapel

Materials Required

Fabric

Black (jacket and hat)	25 x 25 cm	(10 x 10 in)
Black/white stripe	4 x 12 cm	(2 x 4 in)
Black/white spot	7 x 10 cm	(3 x 4 in)
Black/white abstract	6 x 10 cm	(3 x 4 in)
Red	4 x 4 cm	(2 x 2 in)

Double-sided iron-on interlining
Dressmaker's carbon, tracing wheel
Unwaxed greaseproof paper
HB pencil
Cotton to match or highlight

Construction Procedure

Measure out required amounts of fabric. Mark out your pattern pieces and cut approximate squares of each colour.

Cut out similar squares of your double-sided iron-on interlining slightly smaller than your material squares, so it will not stick to your ironing board or iron.

Turn your fabric wrong side up and place your interlining over the material square, sticky side down towards material, paper upwards, making sure there is no overhang. Press with a dry iron.

Place your pattern pieces mirror-reverse onto the paper backing, and trace around your patterns. Now, cut these out.

Using a hard surface and your HB pencil or dressmaker's carbon, trace out the facial lines. Mark lightly where the top mouth line will go and mark in the bottom line slightly darker, just enough for you to see while you stitch.

Place the face, hat, collar, and jacket into approximate position. Once you have ascertained the position, gently remove the paper backing one at a time. (That is, remove the paper from face and put it back into position, then the hat, etc.) Remove the paper backing from hatband and place onto hat, as it is difficult sometimes to see on dark fabrics. The light band will give you a better guideline.

Now place the earrings into position. Just lift the left-hand side (LHS) of the face slightly and slide the edge in a fraction. Place the right earring just under the hat and over the face. Place the tie into position after removing paper backing. Slide the tie edges under the jacket lapels. Place the red knot of tie onto the tie. Lastly place the red mouth into position.

Check that you have removed all paper backing, and nothing has moved. Place unwaxed greaseproof paper over the design, and press with a steam iron, holding down in one position. Lift and press down in another position. Repeat this until you have completely covered the whole design. Do not slide the iron over the design until you are sure the design is completely adhered to the background material.

Place unwaxed greaseproof paper behind your background fabric and prepare your machine for stitching.

Stitching Procedure

Thread your machine with black cotton, and wind your bobbin with black, unless you intend to use white for all colours. (If you set your tension at 3, the white will not show through.)

Starting at the LHS of the hatband, secure thread and, with a stitch width of 3 1/4, slowly stitch over the band to cover the white and come round the crown to the right-hand side (RHS) band. Pivot at corner and come back to the LHS again. Secure thread and stitch the top section of the hatband.

Now, start at the RHS top of the hat, secure thread and stitch down around the hat. Take it slowly as you reach the curve. Pivot regularly around the curve and stitch until you come back to the LHS crown.

Now, come down to the face starting at the right earring. Insert your needle right on the line and stitch around to the LHS. Secure thread. Come down and do the shoulder lines. Pivot at corner and do the peaks of the lapel. Pivot and come down the lapel. Pivot and come across the bottom and back up the LHS in the same manner until you reach the face.

Now, do the tie, securing thread each side of red. Now, do the internal line of lapel securing thread before and after. Now go to the right shoulder and do the collar. Stitch the straight section first, and pivot at the corner. For the curved section, you will need to go slowly and follow your pencil lines exactly.

If you do not get the curve right, unpick it and start again or it will not look as good. Stop at the neckline. Secure thread and repeat the same for the left collar. Now do the neckline. Secure thread at start and finish.

Now, go to the earrings. Get as close as you can to the RHS hat. Secure thread and stitch down to the corner. Pivot and stitch across. Pivot and stitch back to the beginning. Repeat the same for the left earring.

Now, reduce your stitch width back to 2 3/4 and do the eyeline. Secure thread at each end. For the nose, I started in the middle of the right nostril. Secure thread and decrease your stitch width to 2. Hold your garment steady and place your needle in the same hole for two stitches. Stop and decrease your stitch width a touch more and using your slow button, if you have one and very slowly stitch round the nostril. Secure thread.

Repeat the same for the left nostril. You could use a stem stitch and hand-embroider the nostrils. The nostrils are quite noticeable. The first ones I did were only marginally large, but it spoilt the design. I unpicked them and did them smaller. So, start smaller first.

Now, change to red and do the lips. Again you will need to reduce your stitch width right down to 1/2.

Secure thread and gradually increase your stitch width back up to only 2 and then back again. You will need to use your slow button if you have one, and take it steady to get the perfect shape. Unpick it if you are unhappy with it. I went over mine twice to get a more even look. Using a stitch width of 2 tends to give an uneven look.

Note: If you feel that machine stitching the lips is a bit much for you, you can outline the lips in pencil and stem stitch around the outline and if you feel adventurous, you could fill it in with satin stitch. If you have already attempted to machine stitch but are unhappy with the results, unpick it, and carefully remove the red material. If it is still sticking fast leave it for a day or so and try again. It will lift.

APPLIQUÉ ABSTRACT

Appliqué Abstract Master Design

This master design can be used as a pattern. It has been reduced to 50%. See page 11 for instructions on enlarging it to full size.

My abstract appliqué designs began from my passion for collecting all sorts of fabrics. I would often go through a store and buy 20 to 50 cm (8 to 12 in) of anything that appealed to me, not really knowing what I had in mind at the time, but couldn't resist the colours or design.

I found that if a colour or design of fabric grabbed me as soon as I saw it, I would buy it. If I had to think about it and bought it anyway, I almost always never used it. So, if a colour or design is striking enough to catch your eye, buy it and you will find a use for it somewhere.

At first I would only buy 10 cm (4 in) of each colour, but as I found my designs became more complex and larger, I needed larger amounts of at least 20 to 50 cm or 8 to 12 in.

Looking for something different, I decided to pull out anything that would suit an evening appliqué. As my favourite colours are purple, hot pink, and sea green, those were the colours I chose, and as I only had certain amounts left of these colours, I tried putting together what I had. It is a bit like putting together a jigsaw. I put the largest of the colours at the bottom and cut it in a curved line and then placed the next colour behind, trimming the pieces to fit together with a small overlap for later stitching. It began to build up to an interesting and striking design.

It is a lot easier if you have already ironed on the double-sided interlining still needed before you start trimming. It is important to balance your design. So start to bring the colours in the bottom section into the top section.

I so enjoyed creating that design, that I decided to pull out all the gold and silver and lace I could find. I picked through these until I found about three variations of lace, two variations of smooth gold, one gold brocade and a smooth silver, and some silver flowers embroidered on tulle which I cut out and hand-stitched to the silver panel on the left shoulder.

I had chosen a white watermarked taffeta for the back, so I introduced it in panels in the front for balance and to tone down the gold and silver.

But after I had completed the appliqué design before sewing the back and front I found together, I found that the gold was still too strong for my taste. So I unpicked the top stitching of the largest middle gold panel and stitched a panel of lace over the gold and got just the effect I was looking for.

I really can't show you exactly how it is done in a pattern form as the pieces are too large to fit onto the pages of a book, so I have drawn a sample for you as a guideline. You can cut that into four and have it en-larged and piece it back together. This is also an excellent opportunity for you to try your hand at creating your own design.

I suggest that you do not use more than six colours. You could use one colour, but make sure you have different shades, and textures for interest. Move the fabric around until you find they blend in well but form a striking pattern.

Sometimes it is necessary to buy an additional fabric to fit into the design that you have chosen. When designing the purple top I found I had plenty of purple shades, hot pinks and sea greens, but still needed the design texture. So, armed with samples of the colours I had chosen I hunted through my favourite stores, and found the perfect balance, a beautiful silky paisley, in purple, sea green, and a touch of hot pink. It was perfect. I decided to make the skirt from the same fabric and was delighted with the overall effect.

I again chose taffeta for the back fabric. I find that taffeta has the stiffness needed to match the stiffness that the appliqué creates. Because the overall design is a little heavier than the usual appliqué design, it is advisable to choose lightweight fabrics. Silks, satins and taffeta are all excellent fabrics, and I would hesitate to use anything heavier. As you always have a lining (I use a lightweight cotton) that the fabrics are pressed onto, you can use very lightweight fabrics that would not normally be effective.

Abstract design need not be limited to garments. Try picking up the colours of your home in making an abstract appliqué cushion. (You would be able to use a heavier weight here as it does not need to hang.) It is an ideal way to blend in the colours of your home. It would also make an unusual quilt, a little different from the patchwork quilts. It also allows you to use fabrics which are normally too small for double-bed quilts. You are limited only by your imagination

Balance is the key. You need balance of colour, texture, and design. An appliqué of all the same texture can be boring, but introduce a small floral design and it lifts and brightens the entire design.

Small designs suit appliqué very well as you are using only small pieces of each fabric. A large design can sometimes be lost, But then you can go bold and geometrical for a large quilt. The possibilities are endless.

I hope you have as much fun as I have had creating these. The beauty is that each one is entirely different to the next and you get to use up all those pieces of fabric that you have hidden away in the cupboards and under the bed. And think of the hundreds of dollars you will be saving on garments that are original and individual!

INDEX

appliqué foot 4
auto-lock 4

Ballpoint needle 4
beads 6
bobbins 4, 10
buttonhole stitch 7–8

carbon, dressmaker's 5
cardboard 5
chain stitch 8
circles 8–9
colour 5–6
construction 10
   see also   patterns
corduroy 6
corners 9
cotton 6
cross stitch 8
curves 9

decoration 6–7
design
   enlargement 10, 11
   reduction 10, 11
   see also   patterns
             quilts
             wall-hangings
diamanté 7
dressmaker's carbon 5

embroidery 7–8
embroidery foot 4
enlargement, pattern 10, 11
equipment 4–5
   see also   patterns

fabric paint 7
fabrics 6
   see also   patterns
feathers 7
foot, sewing machine 4
French knots 8

greaseproof paper, unwaxed 10
grids 10–11

hints 10

interlining 5, 10
irons 5, 10

leather 6
linen 6

materials *see* equipment
                   fabrics
                   patterns

needles 4

paint, fabric 7
patterns 12–95
   Aeroplane 59–61
   American Raccoon Golf Player
      78–82
   Appliqué Abstract 94–5
   Australian Gumnuts 85–7
   Australian Kangaroo Tennis Player
      62–5
   Australian Koala Basketball Player
      74–7
   Boy's quilt 46
   Bozo the Clown 88–91
   Butterfly 34–6
   Clown Face 28–30
   Dinosaur 46–9
   English Lion Cricket Player 66–70
   Frill–necked Lizard 54–6
   Frog on Toadstool 31–3
   Girl's Quilt 28
   Jet Plane 49–50
   Koala 18–21
   Kookaburra 15–17
   Lady's Face 92–4
   Mr Hippo 51–3
   Mrs Mouse 40–3
   New Zealand Kiwi Football Player
      82–5
   Platypus 24–7
   Pygmy Possum 12–15

Rainbow Lorikeet 22–4
Rupert the Frog 56–9
Tasha the Cat 36–9
Unicorn 43–5
see also   quilts
             wall-hangings
pivot 9–10
polyester satin 6
pressing cloth 5
pressure dial 4

quilts 28, 46

reduction, pattern 10, 11
running stitch 8

satin 6
satin stitch 7
scissors 4–5
sequins 6
sewing machine 4
shapes 8–10
stem stitch 7
stitching 4, 7–10
   see also   circles
             embroidery
             patterns
             pivot
suede 6

Teflon leather foot 4
thread tension 4
tracing wheel 5
transfer pencils 5

Universal needle 4
unpicking 10

wall-hangings
   Australian Native Animal 6, 12
   fabric 6
   International Stars of Sport 62
washing 6
wedge point leather needle 4